THE MASONIC TREASURER

THE MASONIC TREASURER

A. W. NELSON *OBE*

LONDON

LEWIS MASONIC

IAN ALLAN GROUP

© 1988
A. W. Nelson, *OBE*

First published in England 1988
Published by
LEWIS MASONIC
Ian Allan Regalia Ltd, Terminal House
Shepperton, TW17 8AS, who are members of the
Ian Allan Group of companies.

British Cataloguing in Publication Data
Nelson, Alan W.
The Masonic Treasurer
1. Freemasonry—Lodge Management
I. Title
366'.   HS395
ISBN 085318 158 6

Printed in Great Britain by
Latimer Trend & Company Ltd, Plymouth

Contents

About the Author

WBro ALAN NELSON was initiated into the Certified Accountant's Lodge in 1958 together with another Brother initiated at the same time, and was the first Initiate to become its Master. He is a member of several other Lodges and Chapters, and is currently Provincial Grand Treasurer of the Province of West Kent.

He has had a long career in accountancy, becoming a Member of The Chartered Association of Certified Accountants in 1953. He became a member of Council of that body in 1966, and its President in the year 1972/73.

In his work in the accountancy profession he has been a member of The Accounting Standards Committee, and was a member of The Auditing Practices Committee. He has practised as a Certified Accountant for many years, and in the New Year's Honours List of 1988 he was awarded the OBE for services to the profession. Throughout his career he has been very active in technical and research matters relating to accountancy.

Foreword

I WAS DELIGHTED when I heard that a book for the guidance of Lodge Treasurers was being written. It is a gap that has needed to be filled for many years and we are indeed fortunate in West Kent that someone of the status and experience of WBro Alan Nelson has found time to complete this book of instruction and guidance for those concerned with the finances of their Lodges.

It will, I am sure, become the standard work not only for West Kent but for Masonry in general. It will guide and assist Treasurers at all stages of experience and will be used as a work of reference by even the most senior Brethren.

Our thanks are due to WBro Alan Nelson for his hard work in producing this manual and I commend it to all Lodge Treasurers who now have a standard book of reference for the future.

SIMON WALEY, *MA*
Provincial Grand Master
West Kent

Acknowledgements

The Author's thanks are extended to all those Brethren, some of whom are accountants and others not, who have assisted him by reading and commenting upon the text of this book.

A. W. Nelson

Chapter 1

Introduction

ALTHOUGH MUCH HAS been written from time to time about the office of treasurer in a masonic lodge or Chapter, or indeed any of the numerous other Masonic Orders, there would seem to be a need for a small work to bring all these matters together in the form of a manual for the use of treasurers. Apart from the master, the treasurer of a lodge is the only officer whose appointment requires election by the brethren in open lodge, and indeed requires that election to be by secret ballot. Rule 112 of the *Book of Constitutions* is quite clear about this, and the rule requires that the treasurer be elected by ballot on the regular day of election of the Master. The rule further provides for The Grand Master, or Provincial or District Grand Master to grant a dispensation for another brother, not being a regular serving officer, to be elected to discharge the treasurer's duties if the treasurer is ill, or absent, or otherwise not in a position to carry out his duties properly. Where such an election is necessary it should be noted that ten days notice, with a statement that such dispensation has been obtained included on the summons, is required. Thus it is clear that the office of treasurer has great importance in the view of Masonic authority.

The same somewhat stringent requirements do not apply to Provincial Grand Treasurers, and indeed it is simply provided in Rule 68(d) that this officer is to be elected annually. In some Provinces, of course, the office of Provincial Grand Treasurer is something of a sinecure, the work being carried out by the staff of the office. In others the duties are very real. In the case of the Grand Treasurer, the rules for election are somewhat more complicated, and it is provided in Rule 20 that the Grand Treasurer is to be nominated in September from among members of Grand Lodge (normally Past Masters or Past Grand Stewards) who have not previously held office. In normal circumstances there is only one nomination, but in the event of an election for the office of Grand Treasurer a complicated election procedure is provided in rules 20 and 21 of the *Book of Constitutions*. This matter need not detain us here, however, for we are concerned more with those office holders whose appointment entails the detailed work of a treasurer.

It is understood that a lodge secretary who made certain enquiries of Grand Lodge concerning the possible appointment of a Grand Treasurer was informed by a very senior officer that there was no necessity for the Grand Treasurer to be an accountant, indeed one of the most successful of Grand Treasurers had been by profession a gynaecologist. Of course, at Grand Lodge the mundane tasks of record keeping and accounts production are undertaken by the staff under the Grand Secretary, but few lodges, and few treasurers can afford to regard the need to keep proper books and to prepare intelligible annual accounts with such Olympian detachment. Many lodge treasurers are, of course, accountants, and much that appears herein will be familiar to them. If therefore some parts of this book appear to them elementary, the author begs their indulgence. It may well be that few lodge treasurers are so far removed from the mundane world of figures as perhaps a gynaecologist, or indeed a practitioner of some other of the more esoteric branches of medicine, or perhaps other professions, might be expected to be. Nevertheless there are many others from the world of banking and finance who find themselves appointed to this office, and who might welcome some guidance which to an accountant might perhaps seem elementary, but is for them much less familiar. This book is primarily intended to fill this need.

Chapter 2

The Duties of a Treasurer

General

THE DICTIONARY DEFINES a treasurer as a person appointed to look after the funds of a society, company, city or other governing body, and this definition is perhaps as useful as any that might be attempted. 'Looking after the funds' is a phrase which has a wide connotation. It involves collecting the money, arranging for its safe custody, disbursing it in the proper and required manner, recording the various transactions involved, and preparing any necessary reports to the members of the society. It also involves the safeguarding of the financial position of the society. It can scarcely be said that a treasurer has adequately discharged his duties if he has failed to take steps to ensure that the society in question has sufficient funds to meet the obligations which it might from time to time incur. Thus where it is proposed to undertake any significant expenditure, it is within the functions of the treasurer to consider whether there exist sufficient resources to meet it. If not, he must say so, and be prepared either to oppose the expenditure, or to suggest ways in which the proposed costs might be met. Similarly, he will be aware of the ongoing recurring expenses which his society must be prepared to meet each year. It is part of his duty to ensure that the normal recurring income is maintained at a level sufficient to ensure that these expenses can be properly discharged. To this end he will find it necessary to prepare annual budgets, and to monitor expenditure against them to ensure that the available funds are not unexpectedly depleted.

Banking etc

In collecting the funds and arranging for their safe custody, the treasurer should endeavour to ensure that any balances which he might hold are utilised to the best advantage of the society. Thus he should bank the funds promptly, and should seek to ensure that any sums of money not currently required to meet expenses are placed in accounts bearing interest at the most advantageous rates which he is able to arrange. Balances kept on current account at banks should be kept as nearly as possible to the minimum necessary to ensure that bank charges are kept to the minimum, and any other funds should be kept on deposit account or in a building society. There are today, an increasing number of accounts giving cheque writing facilities which at the same time bear interest. It will often be of advantage to investigate these possibilities. In addition many Building Societies offer accounts bearing rates of interest in excess of bank deposit accounts, and many banks offer deposit account facilities at higher rates where the balances can be maintained at a sufficient level.

Disbursement of Funds

The safe custody of the funds at the treasurer's disposal extends to the rules under which those funds are disbursed. It may be, and in the case of Masonic Lodges almost always is, the case that the treasurer has power to make all normal payments, and other extraordinary payments, provided that they are small. Larger extraordinary payments, however, may require special authorisation. In the case of Lodges, such payments must usually be authorised in open lodge after notice on the summons, except in cases of emergency. In the latter case the Master may have power to authorise the payment provided that it is reported at the next regular meeting. Whatever the rules may require, the treasurer should familiarise himself with them and take steps to ensure that there is strict compliance with them. When payments are made they will normally be made by cheque, and in these circumstances it is considered that at least two signatures (the treasurer's and one other) should be required.

Investment

It may be the case in certain wealthier lodges and other societies that there exist funds surplus to the immediate requirements of the body concerned. Such funds should be carefully invested, and it is part of the treasurer's duty of safeguarding the assets within his care, to arrange for this investment. In arranging such investment, the Treasurer should first have regard to the rules of the society. Are there any restrictions placed upon its power to invest its surplus funds? If there are such restrictions, it is the duty of the treasurer to ensure that the powers of investment are not infringed. The next matter which the treasurer must bear in mind in these circumstances is the necessity for prudence. We are all careful to ensure the safety of our own funds, though as individuals we may perhaps from time to time feel able to indulge in a little judicious speculation. A treasurer, in the exercise of his duties, has no such discretion. He must act in such a way as to ensure the safety of the funds under his care. Normally with relatively small sums he will be inclined to restrict himself to government securities. This however need not necessarily be the case where larger sums are involved. Modern investment theory demonstrates that with a sufficiently diversified portfolio of good quality equity shares it is possible to eliminate from the portfolio as a whole all specific risk, leaving only the normal market risk in the portfolio. Thus with a well organised portfolio of ordinary shares, reasonable and proper security of the funds can be ensured. At the same time, investment of this type is very much a matter for the expert, and no treasurer should embark upon this course without the benefit of expert professional advice.

Care of other Assets

In the foregoing paragraphs we have discussed the treasurer's duties in relation to the funds of his society. It must be said, however, that his duties go beyond the necessity to care for the money entrusted to him. Many institutions have other assets. Investments once obtained must be placed in safe-keeping. Share certificates, for example, may be lodged with bankers, as may deeds of any property which the society might own. There are numerous other matters, usually smaller but no less important for that, which must be borne in mind. For example there may be furniture or regalia. The treasurer should satisfy himself that proper arrangements are made for the safety, and where appropriate, the management of such assets. In addition he should take steps to ensure that they are adequately covered by insurance. In this connection it is sometimes the case that cover is provided by another institution. For example a society may hold its meetings in premises owned by another organisation. The fire cover held in relation to these premises may extend to all the contents, in which case the society concerned may feel able to rely on this. If so, well and good, but the treasurer should satisfy himself on this point. If premises are owned they should be covered not only for fire and similar risks, but also for those risks attendant upon property ownership. The treasurer should make a point of ensuring not only that all these risks are covered, but that the cover is adequately reviewed. Thus the treasurer should regard himself, insofar as the rules permit, as the custodian of the assets of the society, and should seek to ensure that they are safeguarded as if they were his own.

Applying all these general principles, therefore, to the Masonic Treasurer we find his duties set out in rule 153 of the *Book of Constitutions*. This rule provides the following:

(1) All monies due to or held for the Lodge should be paid or remitted to the Treasurer.

(2) The treasurer should pay such funds into an account in the name of the Lodge.

(3) The bank used must be approved by resolution of the lodge.

(4) The treasurer must make those payments which are duly authorised or sanctioned by the Lodge.

(5) All cheques must be signed by the Treasurer and (unless the Lodge resolves otherwise) by at least one other member authorised by the Lodge.

(6) The Treasurer must enter all such transactions in the books, which are the property of the Lodge.

(7) When another Treasurer is appointed in his stead he must transfer all funds and the books to his successor.

The rule in question contains further detailed requirements pertaining to the preparation of annual accounts and audit. It is, however, intended to deal with these matters at a later stage, and accordingly they are not further elaborated here. It will, however, be readily seen that the general discussion in the above paragraphs is entirely in accord with the requirements of rule 153, and the requirements for Treasurers generally are in no way different for a Masonic Lodge.

The Duties as applied to Freemasonry

We have described generally the duties of a treasurer in a variety of institutions, because in these respects the duties of a Masonic treasurer closely parallel these general requirements. The Masonic treasurer will have regard to the rules set out in the *Book of Constitutions*, the byelaws of his lodge, and the requirements of his brethren expressed in open lodge. Within these parameters his concerns will be no different from those which exercise the treasurers of a wide variety of voluntary organisations, and his duty of care owed to the brethren of his lodge will be the same.

Chapter 3

The Books of Account

Some Elementary Considerations

SOME CONSIDERABLE THOUGHT has been given to the question of the level of
theoretical book-keeping knowledge which a work of this nature should
assume to be possessed by readers. Obviously many of those elected to the
office of treasurer will be accountants or possessed of some accountancy
training, and these may be assumed to have expert knowledge of the
subject. The temptation, therefore, is to plunge straight into a discussion of
the books and records to be kept without attempting any preliminary
explanation of the principles involved. At the same time, it must not be
forgotten that some, at least, will have nothing more to bring to the task
than an ability to carry out the necessary arithmetic, together with a
willingness and desire to be of help to their fellows, perhaps reinforced by
some general commercial experience. It may perhaps be said that the
greater the level of expertise possessed by the treasurer, the less regard he
need have to this little book, and the converse is certainly true. In these
circumstances therefore, it is felt that on balance some explanation at a
very elementary level may first be desirable. For those who have no need of
such simple instruction apologies are tendered, but they can at least omit
the offending paragraphs and move on to what, for them, may be more
useful sections of the work.

The Double Entry Principle

The only system of book-keeping which can be considered to be a complete
and fully developed system, is that which goes by the name of 'Double
Entry Book-keeping'. Single entry systems are merely methods of recording

individual transactions, mainly cash and bank transactions in books in such a way that they can be used and understood. Such systems cannot be considered complete, and while it may be possible to construct a simple Receipts and Payments Account therefrom, a proper Income and Expenditure Account together with a Balance Sheet requires the application of double entry principles, and where necessary, the conversion of single entry records to a double entry version. What then, is double entry book-keeping? It is a system of book-keeping which recognises and records the fact that every transaction has two sides. For example if *A* buys some goods from *B* and pays *B* cash for these goods we can look at these transactions in the following way:

> *A* has acquired some goods and divested himself of some cash.
> *B* has divested himself of some goods and acquired some cash.

Both *A*'s books and *B*'s books will record both sides of these transactions, but each from his own point of view. Thus the books of both will have means of recording both receipts and divestiture of both goods and cash. These two aspects of transactions are recorded on the debit (left hand) side of the books for receipts, and the credit (right hand) side for divestiture or payment. They will also require two types of account designated Nominal Accounts and Personal Accounts. In the books of *A* his own side of the transaction will appear in his Nominal Accounts and *B*'s side will appear in a Personal Account relating to *B*. The reverse will apply to *B*'s books. Thus taking the individual transactions, *A*'s acquisition of goods will appear in a Nominal Account, probably designated 'Purchases' in his books while he will open a Personal Account for *B* which will record the fact on the credit side that *B* has disposed of the goods in question. Similarly *A*'s Cash Book will record on the credit side his expenditure of the money, and this same money will be recorded in *B*'s Personal Account on the debit side as cash received. In the case of *B*, precisely the opposite will occur. *B* will record his disposal of goods in his own Nominal Account designated 'Sales' on the credit side and will record the receipt of those same goods in a Personal Account for *A* on the debit side. Similarly he will record the cash received on the debit of his Cash Book, posting this same cash to his Personal Account for *A* on the credit side.

These facts explain a matter which some people find puzzling about bank statements. 'Why?' they ask 'if the receipts side of the books is the debit, do my bank statements show all my receipts on the credit side?' The answer, of course, is that the bank produces to its customer a copy of that customer's account *as it appears in the books of the bank*. Thus when the customer pays money into his bank, from the bank's point of view it is receiving cash, and its customer is paying that money out. Thus the money banked appears as a credit in the customer's account.

The Books of Account and their Use

The intention of any book-keeping system is to record, analyse and classify receipts and expenses in such a way that they may be conveniently aggregated and summarised in financial statements which will convey useful information to the reader. Thus the object of the masonic treasurer is to record the receipts and payments of his lodge in such a way that for each financial year he can show the receipts and payments summarised under appropriate heads to explain how the lodge has received and disposed of its income, and what in the outcome is its financial position.

In double entry book-keeping, the books are classified into two general classes.

These are   (1) Books of Prime Entry.
                          (2) Ledgers.

Books of Prime Entry

These are books in which a transaction is first recorded, and it may be said that they are covered by the following:

    (1) Cash Books (including petty cash books).

(2) Day Books.

(3) The Journal.

We shall here be concerned mainly with Cash Books, but it may be of general assistance to describe briefly the use of Day Books and the Journal so that the reader may have a more complete picture. The term 'day book' is to some extent self-explanatory. Day books are books, normally in use from day to day, which are used to record a particular type or class of transaction. For example all sales of goods by a business whose trade consisted in such sales, if sales on credit, would normally give rise to a sales invoice. Such sales invoices would be recorded, normally in numerical order, in a Sales Day book. At the end of the accounting period adopted (weekly, monthly or annually) the book is totalled and the total of the sales for the period is posted to the credit side of the Sales Account in the ledger. Nominal Accounts such as Sales and Purchases are usually kept in a special 'Nominal Ledger'. The individual invoices entered in the Sales Day book are posted to separate accounts for each customer on the debit side of the Sales Ledger which normally contains the personal sales accounts. Similarly the purchase of goods for resale will be the subject of a purchase invoice. Such invoices are normally entered into a Purchase Day book which is similarly totalled periodically, the totals being posted to the debit side of a Purchases Account, while the individual items are posted to the credit side of the personal accounts in a Purchase Ledger. It will be noted that the entries in the sales account are on the credit side, indicating that the business in question has disposed of the goods, while the individual sales ledger accounts, having the entries on the debit side, indicate the acquisition of goods by the customer. Similarly the Purchases Account, being posted to the debit, indicates the acquisition of goods for resale, while the individual Purchase Ledger postings, being to the credit of suppliers accounts, indicate the disposal by the individual suppliers of those goods.

It will be further noted that the totals of sales or Purchases being posted to their respective accounts will be exactly balanced arithmetically by the individual entries in the respective ledgers. Thus if the work is done correctly and both sides of the books are added up, the totals will be equal on either side. Below is an illustration of a typical day book.

Fig 1

1. Date 1987	Details	Ledger Folios	No.	£	p	£	p
Jan 1	A. Abel 30 Widgets	1	1	30	–		
	25 Under Widgets			12	50	42	50
Jan 24	B. Baker 17 Spludgeons	2	2	4	25		
	12 Wotnots				24	4	49
						46	99
						N/L	1

Very often the detail in the first cash column would be omitted and a single cash column, with a single line for each entry would be used. Upon the assumption that the above is an illustration of a Sales Day Book, the ledger postings consequent upon these transactions would be as shown in the illustration (*fig 2*).

The Ledger

The ledger is the principal book of record in double entry book-keeping. In our discussion of the books of prime entry we have referred to the debit and credit sides of the ledger. There are different rulings for ledgers, some showing debits, credits and balances in separate columns as for example bank statements. We shall, however, be concerned with the normally ruled ledger which is as illustrated (*fig 2*).

We have already seen that the debit side of the ledger records receipts or incomings and the credit side payments or outgoings. Thus in personal ledgers, the individual accounts of suppliers or customers would record goods received or disposed of and cash paid by them or received by them, while the nominal accounts would record the other side of the transaction from the point of view of the organisation whose books they were. Both nominal and personal ledgers are ruled in the same way. Thus if the illustrated ledger (*fig 2*) were used as a Sales ledger, the goods sold to the customer would appear as debits in his account, and when he paid for them, the payments would appear as credits, whereas in the nominal ledger, the sales account would show the sales on the outgoing or credit side, and the debit side of the cash book would record the cash received.

Fig 2

THE LEDGER

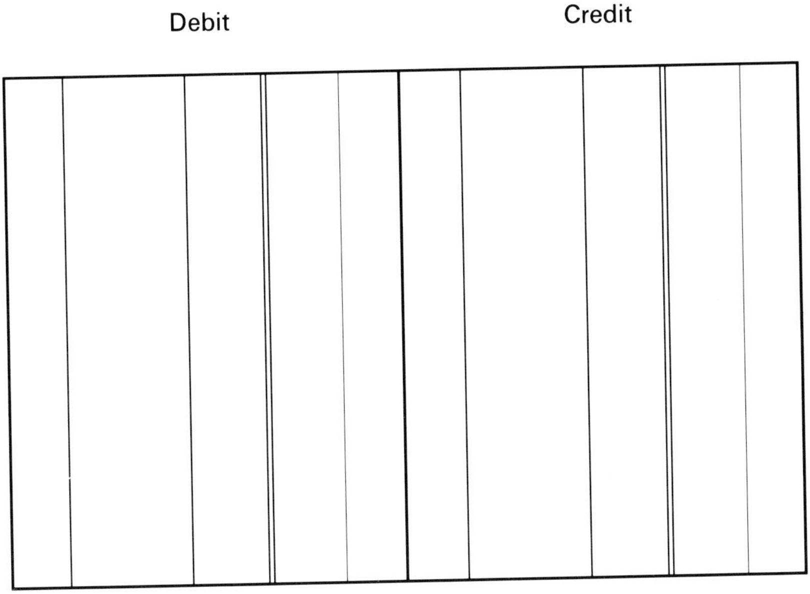

Debit   Credit

We may now turn again to the sales to A. Abel and B. Baker illustrated above (*fig 1*) and we see that the sales account in the nominal ledger, and the personal accounts in the sales ledger will be as follows. (*figs 3* and *4*)

Had the day book illustrated been a Purchase Day Book, all the ledger entries would have been reversed. For example the Sales Account would

Fig 3

NOMINAL LEDGER
Sales Account

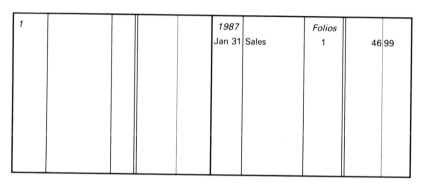

1					1987		Folios			
					Jan 31	Sales	1		46	99

Fig 4

SALES LEDGER

1 1987 Jan 1	Goods	SDB 1	A. Abel 42	50						
2 1987 Jan 24	Goods	1	B. Baker 4	49						

have been the Purchases Account, and the total of £46.99 would have been posted to the debit side of the account, and the individual personal accounts would have been Purchase Ledger accounts, with the entries for goods on the credit side.

The Journal

The journal is a book which the treasurer will seldom encounter. It is used to record exceptional items, and the entries are made in two cash columns to indicate to which side in the ledger accounts affected the relevant entries should be posted. A journal entry might be made in a commercial set of books, for example, to write off a bad debt. A journal and such an entry are shown below (*fig 5*).

Fig 5

JOURNAL

1							
1987							
June 30	Bad Debts Account	N/L 3		4	49		
	B. Baker	S/L 2				4	49
	Bad Debt written off						

If we now assume the accounts as above, B. Baker's account will now appear as follows:

Fig 6

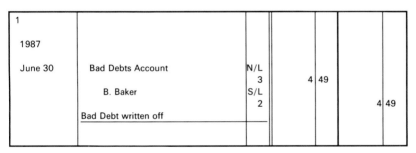

2						1987					2
1987						B. Baker					
Jan 24	Goods	1		4	49	June 30	Bad Debts Account	J/1		4	49

The Nominal Ledger will now have an account for the bad debt written off.

Fig 7

3				BAD DEBTS							3
1987											
June 30	B. Baker	J/1		4	49						

It will be noted that the entries in the journal are posted to the same side in the ledger, that is to say the debit in the journal is posted to the debit of the ledger and vice versa. Many years ago the journal was the principal book of prime entry, and all items to be posted to the ledger were first entered therein. With the development of commerce in the last two or three hundred years, however, this was highly inconvenient, and frequently recurring entries were removed into specialised books: hence the development of Sales and Purchases Day Books, sometimes referred to as Sales and Purchase Journals.

The Cash Book

We said earlier that we should mainly be concerned with the cash book as a book of prime entry. The cash book is usually subdivided, with one book relating to the bank account, and one to cash or petty cash items. In more complex cases, for example where there is more than one bank account, there may well be more than one cash book, but we need not consider such cases except to observe that in complex cases the rules are no different than for the simple case. The simple cash book is in reality a specialised ledger

Fig 8

CASH BOOK

Debit   **Credit**

account and is part of the Nominal Ledger. A specimen ruling of such a book is shown above, (*fig 8*), from which it will be noted that it differs in no way from the ledger accounts illustrated.

It should, however, be noted that the cash book will normally be ruled so that when opened, the debit side occupies the left hand page and the credit side the right hand page. Very often the cash book will have two cash columns, so that it will be ruled like the journal illustrated above. In such cases, the right hand column on each page will normally be used to record entries passing through the bank account, that is to say, amounts paid in on the debit side, and cheques drawn on the credit side. The other cash column may have several uses. In commercial books it may, for example be used to record cash discounts taken or given. A second use would be to record the cash (as opposed to bank) account in cases where cash transactions were few and a separate cash book or petty cash book was not considered necessary. Alternatively it could be used to analyse personal and nominal ledger items.

Before we proceed further it may be sensible to consider the simple cash book illustrated above, in use.

Fig 9

CASH BOOK

Debit					Credit			
1 1987 Jan 14	A. Abel	SL/1	42	50				1

SALES LEDGER

1987		SDB			A. ABEL		CB/		
Jan 14	Goods	1	42	50	Jan 14	Bank	1	42	50

When we were considering the sales day book we recorded a sale to A. Abel of £42.50 goods sold. The above cash book entry records the payment for those goods. It will be noted that A. Abel's account now balances, as indeed did the account of B. Baker after we had written off the bad debt through the Journal. If we now extracted the balances from the books after all these transactions we should find the following position:

Fig 10

			Dr		Cr	
	Cash at Bank		42	50		
	Bad Debt		4	49		
	Sales				46	99
	Total		46	99	46	99

The above is, of course, a very simple example of a trial balance.

It will be noted that in posting the cash book entries, those on the debit side of the cash book are posted to the credit side of the ledger. We saw above that the cash book is in reality a specialised nominal ledger account, and we can now set out the main rules to be observed when posting entries to the ledger. These are:

(1) *Postings in the ledger are posted across* ie if an original entry is a debit it is posted to the credit and vice versa. This holds good for the day books also, for if we give the position a little thought we shall see that the total of the Sales Day Book is posted to the credit of the sales account, and the individual items are posted to the debit of the Sales Ledger personal accounts, while the reverse holds true for the Purchases Day Book.

(2) *Every debit must have a credit, and every credit a debit.* This is known as 'The Golden Rule of Book-keeping' and every trained book-keeper has the rule always in mind. The reader should try to train himself to think in this way. By doing so he will avoid the problem of one-sided entries, and the consequent difficulties in balancing his books.

The Analysed Cash Book

It will be seen from the foregoing remarks that with the aid of the books discussed most quite complex financial transactions can be easily recorded. The problem that arises is that in posting ledgers with individual accounts for each member, the treasurer of a voluntary organisation can find himself saddled with a considerable amount of work, and also with considerable scope for error in posting his personal accounts. Usually, however, many of the entries to be made in his books are repetitive and may also involve standard amounts of money. In a masonic lodge, for example, receipts will normally consist of annual subscriptions, Initiation and Joining fees, and dining charges. The benevolent or charity receipts should be accounted for separately and kept in a separate account, and we will come to this later. Expenses will similarly fall into certain standard and repetitive classes. For example, these will be costs of temple hire, dining charges, stationery and secretarial expenses, dues to Grand Lodge and Provincial or District Grand Lodge, costs of regalia and the like. By using an analysed cash book, having special columns for the recording of each class of receipt or payment, we can largely reduce, and in some cases perhaps even eliminate the necessity to keep a nominal ledger. A personal ledger, containing an account for each member of the lodge may be maintained, but by using a members register this too can be eliminated, so that the main books to be kept would be the analysed cash book, the members register, and perhaps a nominal ledger. We shall proceed on the basis that a nominal ledger is maintained, though later in the discussion we will see how it might be eliminated in suitable circumstances.

The following is a typical example of an analysed cash book having six columns on the debit side and twelve columns on the credit side. Such books vary, having perhaps only three or four debit columns, but sometimes more than five, and perhaps fourteen or more credit columns.

The choice of ruling is dictated by the extent of the analysis required, and in our case this would probably depend upon the number of income and expenditure items in the final accounts of the lodge. At this point it may perhaps be pertinent to say that it is not absolutely necessary to have a different column for every item. Some items may occur very few times, perhaps only once, in a year. For example a lodge may have only one or

Fig 11

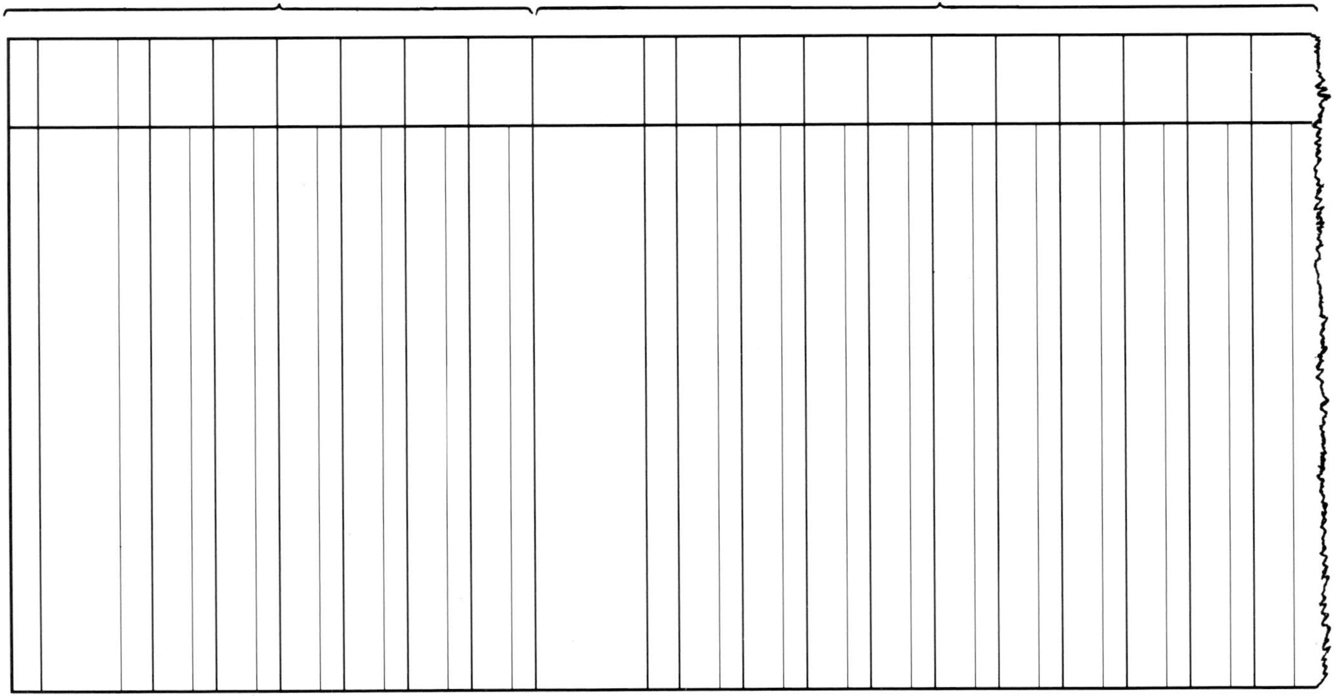

two initiates each year. In such a case it would be perfectly acceptable to include both initiation fees and subscriptions in the same column, and to analyse the total of the column between the two types of receipt at the end of the year. Dues to Grand Lodge and Provincial or District Grand Lodge may be similarly treated, as indeed may some other classes of expenditure.

We may now consider in practice the use of a book of this nature, and accordingly the heads to be adopted for each of the columns. In deciding this we need to consider the end result which we wish to produce, and this will be governed by the items which we anticipate will be individually reported in the annual accounts which we shall prepare. Let us therefore consider a typical lodge Balance Sheet and Income and Expenditure Account. On the income side we would expect to find the following items:

Initiation, Joining and Rejoining Fees
Subscriptions
Dining Receipts

On the expenditure side the following items might be expected:

Dues to Grand Lodge
Dues to Provincial or District Grand Lodge
Temple Hire Costs
Regalia and Rituals
Printing Postage and Stationery
Dining Charges
Miscellaneous Expenses
Tyler's Fees

In these circumstances we might expect to head the columns of our analysed cash book as depicted in *fig* 12.
We may now note the following points:

1. *Contra Columns*

There are sometimes entries which affect both sides of the books. The main such item is the balance when we rule off the cash book at the end of a period. If there is a balance in hand, this will be entered on the credit side of the period just ended, and carried down to the debit side of the new period. Each entry in the cash book will be entered in the 'bank' column, which is of course a total column, and extended to one of the subsidiary columns. In this way the totals can be proved, since the totals of the subsidiary columns added together will equal the total of the bank column. The balance will be entered in the contra column on either side.

2. *Bank Columns*

As indicated above, these are total columns. Very often the bank column will be the first column on the debit and not the last as in the illustration. This is merely a matter of personal preference. In the illustration the format adopted has been chosen so that the columns recording bank receipts and bank payments are close together and can be more easily related.

3. *Miscellaneous*

It will be noted that two columns have been utilised for this heading. One column will be used to record the cash and the other for annotation purposes. We shall later consider the analysed cash book in use, but before we proceed to this further stage it would, perhaps, be as well to proceed to the consideration of the members register, and this will record items relating to individual lodge members.

The Members Register

We have already seen that a book-keeping system based upon the ledger and subsidiary books would be perfectly capable of handling any normal financial recording problem. The ledger does, however, present a difficulty in that it presupposes a personal account for every customer, or in the case of a lodge, for every member. This would involve entering each transaction in some form of day book, and posting these transactions to individual ledger accounts. The cash received would then be posted to the credit side

Fig 12

Debit

Date	Details	Initiation Joining Rejoining	Sub-scriptions	Dining	Contra	Bank	Date	Details	Bank

Credit

Grand Lodge		Provincial Grand Lodge		Temple Hire		Regalia Etc		Printing Postage and Stationery		Dining		Tyler		Contra		Miscellaneous	

to balance the account, and any remaining balances would indicate unpaid dues of one sort or another. This, it will readily be seen, would involve considerable work to record numerous transactions which were essentially similar in character. This similarity fortunately enables us to devise a method of reducing the amount of work by eliminating the necessity for posting a ledger. A little thought shows us that members of a lodge have a very limited class of transactions with their lodge. They pay an Initiation or Joining fee, an annual subscription, and dining charges. These charges are paid once for the Initiation or Joining fee, once a year for the subscription, and once for each meeting at which a member dines or has guests. By designing a register with one line for each member, and one column for each transaction the ledger can be eliminated. Depending upon the number of transactions per member to be recorded annually, we can expect to incorporate two or three years, or possibly more, of transactions across a single page of an analysis book. Such a register is illustrated below

Fig 13

MEMBERS REGISTER

Name	Arrears B/F		Current Subs.		September	November	January	March	May	Arrears B/F
		pd.		pd.	pd.	pd.	pd.	pd.	p.d	pd.
A. Abel	25.00	8/9	8.50	8/9						
B. Baker	25.00	8/9	17.00	8/9						
C. Charley	25.00	8/9	8.50	8/9						

Each line is used to record the transactions relating to one member, and the record of his dues and dining charges is entered across the page using the £ column to record cost. The pence column is used to note the date payment is received. Any items not so dated will represent outstanding sums due.

The Analysed Cash Book in Use: Appendix 1 shows the completed books for a year for a lodge having fifteen members, and the reader is urged to trace through each of the entries therein to familiarise himself with the methods of book-keeping used. At this point, however, we shall discuss briefly how the analysed cash book is kept. It will be noted that entries for two members A. Abel and B. Baker have been shown in the above illustration of the Members Register. We may now see how the payment of these dues is recorded in the analysed cash book. We shall also look at one or two other entries relating to payments for Grand Lodge dues, dining charges and the payment of the Tyler. It will be noted from *fig 14* that the Tyler is assumed to have been paid in cash on the evening of the meeting (8th September). The cash used for this purpose is assumed to have been part of the payment assumed to come from C. Charley. Provided enough cash was in fact received for this purpose, (ie at least £8.00) it could be assumed to have been paid by any member who actually paid in cash. C. Charley is shown as having made two payments, namely one of £25.50 which forms part of the amount of £101.00 paid into the bank, and one of £8.00. This latter sum, although entered in the bank column was not in fact banked, but was handed to the Tyler. This is recorded on the credit or payments side of the cash book, and is also entered in the bank column, though of course it was not in fact drawn from the bank. This does not matter, however, for the two entries of £8.00 in the bank column cancel out and the bank will be unaffected. It is however necessary to enter these amounts in this way, since otherwise the cross-casts of the entries will not agree. For the purposes of illustration, the book has been balanced after these few entries, and the balance carried down. It will be noted that on each side of the book, the totals of the subsidiary columns equal the total of the bank column, thus proving the arithmetical accuracy of the entries made. If we now turn back to the illustration of the members register (*fig 13*) we may note that the date 8/9 has been entered against each item indicating the date payment was received. One further point to note is that the column immediately after the details on the payment side of the cash book, has been used to record the last three numbers of the cheques drawn. This is a useful practice, and can be of considerable assistance when reconciling the cash book and bank statements.

Fig 14

Date	Details		Initiation Joining Rejoining		Sub-scriptions	Dining	Contra	Bank	Date	Details	Cheque No	Bank
Sep 1 8	Balance	B/F					450 00	450 00	Sep 2 8	Grand Lodge–Fees	014	65 57
	A Abel				25 00	8 50				Good & Lo butchers	015	118 80
	B Baker				25 00	17 00				Tylers Fee (in cash)	¢	8 00
	C Charley				25 00	50		101 00		Balance	C/D	366 63
		¢				8 00		8 00				
					75 00	34 00	450 00	559 00				559 00
9	BALANCE	B/D					366 63	366 63				

Grand Lodge	Provincial Grand Lodge	Temple Hire	Regalia	Printing Postage and Stationery	Dining	Tyler	Contra		Miscellaneous	
65 57					118 80	8 00	366 63			
65 57					118 80	8 00	366 63			

The Bank Reconciliation

We noted when dealing with the elementary considerations that the bank statements were a copy of the customers personal account with the bank, and for this reason amounts paid in to the bank are shown as credits, whereas cheques drawn and other payments are shown as debits. This, as we noted is the opposite way round to the way in which the customer himself will record the transactions concerned in his own cash book.

Bank Statements are today prepared by computer, and the design of the statement itself has developed both to accommodate more readily the requirements of automation, and also to indicate after each transaction the balance remaining on the account. The following is an illustration of a typical bank statement today.

Fig 15

UNIVERSAL BANK PLC			STATEMENT OF ACCOUNT	
Details	Payments	Receipts	Date	Balance

Figure 16 above shows such a simple cash book with its attendant bank statement. In reconciling the cash book with the bank statements the first step is to draw a line on the bank statement beneath the date at which we wish to agree the two records. In this example the line is drawn after the 28th January 1987, there being no further entries before the 31st of that month. We next tick off the cash book entries against those appearing in the bank statements. Note how the cash book record of the final three numbers on each cheque is of assistance in identifying the relevant entries in the

Fig 16

CASH BOOK							
1987			1987				
Jan 1	Paid in to open Account	200 00 \	Jan 5	Self	001	25 00 \	
7	B. Jones	50 00 \	10	K. James	002	119 27 \	
12	P. South	45 00 \	18	L. Adams	003	28 98 \	
15	A. Brown	12 17 \	25	R. Perkins	004	68 22 \	
23	R. Amos	158 20 \	29	M. Wilson	005	101 00 o/s	
30	Overseas Traders	189 00 o/s	31	P. Richards	006	27 80 o/s	
				Balance	c/d	284 10 ₵	
		£654 37				£654 37	
Feb 1	Balance B/d	284 10 ₵					

UNIVERSAL BANK PLC

STATEMENT OF ACCOUNT
31 Jan 87
No. 1

DETAILS		PAYMENTS	RECEIPTS	DATE	BALANCE
				1987	
COUNTER CREDIT			200 00 \	1 JAN	200 00
	200001	25 00 \		5 JAN	175 00
COUNTER CREDIT			50 00 \	7 JAN	225 00
	200002	119 27 \		13 JAN	105 73
BGC			45 00 \	13 JAN	150 73
COUNTER CREDIT			12 17 \	16 JAN	162 90
	200003	28 98 \		22 JAN	133 92
COUNTER CREDIT			158 20 \	24 JAN	292 12
	200004	68 22 \		28 JAN	223 90
BGC			189 00	1 FEB	412 90
	200005		101 00	4 FEB	311 90
	200006		27 80	4 FEB	284 10
ABBREVIATIONS:	DIV: Dividend		STO: Standing Order		
	BGC: Bank Giro Credit		DR: Overdrawn		

bank statement. The next step is to mark the outstanding items thus o/s. The balance carried down is marked thus,¢. It is useful to mark each figure this way because this helps to ensure that no items are overlooked. We may now prepare our bank reconciliation statement as follows:

Fig 17

BANK RECONCILIATION STATEMENT

1987					
Jan 31	**Balance at Bank per Statement**				223 90
	Add Banking not yet credited				
	Overseas Traders				189 00
					412 90
	Deduct Outstanding Cheques				
	M. Wilson	005	101 00		
	P. Richards	006	27 80		128 80
Jan 31	Balance per Cash Book				£284 10

The bank reconciliation statement as shown above should be retained, and the outstanding items checked through into the following period. This will also assist the auditors in verifying the bank account.

A Completed set of Books—Notes

In Appendix 1 there is shown a complete members register, analysed cash book and nominal ledger for an imaginary lodge, the Exborough Lodge. The annual accounts are in Appendix 3. It is suggested that before reading further, readers may find it helpful to familiarise themselves, and perhaps work through this simple example. One or two points should be noticed in working through these figures as follows:

1.   The members register shows subscriptions paid for the year of £300 and subscriptions due at the year end of £50. This agrees with the total of £350 for the year shown in the income and expenditure account (Appendix 3).

2.   The members register shows dining receipts collected of £976.50 and outstandings of £25.50. This agrees with the cash received for dining shown in the income and expenditure account of £1002.00 (Appendix 3).

3.   The total of arrears in the members register agrees with the debtors figure in the balance sheet (Appendix 3).

4.   The dates of receipt of the various sums paid by members have been entered against the relevant items in the Members Register.

5.   The unpaid amounts carried forward in the members register are marked o/s (outstanding).

6.   The contra column in the analysed cash book has been used to record the balance brought forward and carried forward. The contras are analysed and agreed after the book is totalled.

7.   The items in the Miscellaneous column are annotated.

8.   The Tyler was paid a fee of £8.00 in cash at the March meeting. This is entered in the bank column, and the receipt for A. Abel has been divided between the amount actually banked, and a separate amount of £8.00 utilised to pay the Tyler. Neither amount will actually pass through the bank, but this will not affect the bank account, because the entries cancel each other. It is necessary to enter the items this way in order to record both the full takings and the payment to the Tyler, while at the same time keeping the columns in agreement.

9.   In January E. Eagle made a payment to the treasurer for some item or other of ritual which was obtained for him. The entry is in the contra column since it does not affect the affairs of the lodge.

10.   At the May meeting £30 was paid into the account which related to the Benevolent Fund. This was the subject of a cheque to that fund, and is also passed through the contra column.

11.   In the ledger, the opening balances brought forward are the shares in the Masonic Hall company purchased in 1985, the debtor of £20.00 for last years subscription for H. Henry (see Members Register) and the Accumulated Fund of £970. These together with the opening bank balance are in effect the opening balance sheet from last year and balance out.

12.   Nothing is shown in the Insurance Account at this point, because the £2.00 due has not yet been paid. It appears as a creditor in the extended trial balance (Appendix 2).

Chapter 4

The Annual Accounts

The Masonic Rules

WE REFERRED IN CHAPTER 2 to the requirements of rule 153 of the *Book of Constitutions* as to the treasurers' duties. As was indicated there, that rule continues by requiring the treasurer to prepare 'a statement of accounts annually'. Such account is to be prepared to a date 'to be determined by the members' and is required to show 'the exact financial position of the lodge'. It is further stated that the accounts must 'be verified and audited by a Committee of Members of the Lodge', and the audit committee is required to be elected annually. The duties of the audit committee are indicated in the requirement that a certificate is to be signed by that committee indicating 'that all balances have been checked and that the accounts have been duly audited'. There is the further requirement that a copy of the accounts bearing this certificate must be sent to all members of the lodge with the summons convening the meeting at which they are to be considered. This meeting must not be later than the third after the accounting date. It should be noted that the rule also requires the books to be available for inspection in open lodge at that meeting, a requirement which today is often more honoured in the breach than the observance though the books should be available if required. The rule also provides for this making of the books available for inspection on any other occasion when the lodge so resolves. Let us then summarise these requirements. They are:

(1) Annual Accounts are to be prepared at a date to be determined by the lodge.

(2) Such accounts must show the exact financial position of the lodge.

(3) The accounts must be audited by a committee required to check all balances.

(4) The audited accounts must be sent to all the members with the appropriate summons.

(5) The meeting to consider the accounts must be not later than the third meeting after the accounting date.

There is also the requirement that the books be made available for inspection, and it should be noted that all these requirements are extended to any other funds maintained in connection with the lodge, whether maintained by the Treasurer or other officers. Examples are given as follows: Benevolent Funds, the funds of Charity or Benevolent Associations, Dining Funds, Charity Box collections 'or other moneys receivable from individual members of the lodge or any of its Officers.'

The principal rule with which we are concerned is, of course, number 2 above which requires an account to show the exact financial position of the lodge. The financial position of any organisation at a given point in time is best shown by a balance sheet. Unfortunately accountants would today argue that the word 'exact' is most inappropriate when applied to a balance sheet or indeed the accompanying Income and Expenditure Account. (This term is used in connection with such accounts of voluntary organisations in preference to the term 'Profit and Loss' Account, which has commercial connotations). Accounts necessarily contain estimates. Creditors, for example, although known to exist may not be capable at the date of the accounts, of precise assessment. Similarly stocks, eg bar stocks are at a valuation, and this may be imprecise. It would seem likely that the somewhat archaic wording of the rule was first devised at a time when Receipts and Payments Accounts (simple statements of cash received and cash paid) were considered adequate, and could be drafted in exact terms. Such accounts, however, are today recognised as inadequate in most cases, and although they may be sufficient to comply with the strict wording of rule 153, we shall consider the preparation of an annual Income and Expenditure Account and Balance Sheet. It should, however, be noted that in the case of simple charity funds which merely receive and disburse money on a small scale, the simple Receipts and Payments Account may be perfectly adequate, since it will detail the receipts and their nature or source, and will indicate the nature of the disbursement made, and in addition will detail the opening and closing Cash or Bank balances. A balance sheet in such circumstances would not be helpful, unless the Benevolent Fund was possessed of other assets such as investments.

The Preparation of Final Accounts

We may now turn to consideration of the Income and Expenditure Account and Balance Sheet, and the methods to be used in their preparation. The idea of a Balance Sheet where both sides (or in the statement form, the top half and the bottom half) add up to the same total is both mystifying and a little frightening to the lay man. It need not be so, however. In the Income and Expenditure Account we shall enter those items from our books of account which represent the income of the year and the expenses incurred in earning that income. In book-keeping parlance we shall 'write off' all the income and expenses to the Income and Expenditure Account. This means that no balances will remain on those accounts unless they relate to sums of money which relate to, and must therefore be carried forward to, the next period. We shall find that all the income lies on the credit side of the ledger, and all the expenses on the debit side. At this point the reader should refer briefly to the simple trial balance (No. 1) in Appendix 2 when the truth of this statement will at once be apparent. Only ledger items 12 and 13 together with the bank balance are excluded from this general statement, and these are not Income and Expenditure items, they are Balance Sheet items. This brings us to the Balance Sheet, and it can now be seen that the term Balance Sheet is an exact description, for the items included therein are those balances remaining after everything else has been written off to the Income and Expenditure Account. The Balance Sheet in short is a list of balances showing what we have, and what we owe, and the net total of these balances, properly stated, is our net worth.

If we again refer to the simple trial balance (1) in Appendix 2 we can see that the debit balance sheet items, the shares in the Exborough Masonic Hall Company and the bank balance are both assets, and the credit item, the Accumulated Fund is our Capital or net worth. This item is adjusted each year by adding to it or deducting from it, as the case may be, the surplus or deficiency shown up by the Income and Expenditure Account. We can now classify the balances shown in our books at the year end before the Income and Expenditure Account and Balance Sheet have been prepared.

Debit balances are:

(1) Assets
(2) Expenses
(3) Losses

Credit balances are:

(1) Liabilities
(2) Gains
(3) Capital

The simple trial balance (1) has been prepared by extracting from the ledger in Appendix 1 the balances, and listing them under the debit or credit columns as they appear in the ledger. We also include the bank balance which is a debit, since it will be recalled that we saw in our discussion on the books of account, that the cash book is in reality a specialised ledger account.

The Extended Trial Balance

In preparing an Income and Expenditure Account and the accompanying Balance Sheet it is necessary to take account of any sums which may be receivable, but have not been received at the accounting date, and also any sums which may be due to others, but which at the accounting date remain unsettled. These amounts are called debtors and creditors respectively (in American parlance 'receivables' and 'payables'). In addition, some payments may have been made which relate wholly or partly to the following period, and some amounts may have been received wholly or partly in advance. As an example we may consider a payment of rent. Let us assume that rent is payable in advance for the following year on the 1st of January.

Let us further assume that the accounts are made up to the 30th June annually. On the 1st January 1987 we pay annual rent of £1000. Of this sum only £500 relates to the year ended 30th June 1987. The remaining £500 we must carry forward as a prepayment to the year ended 30th June 1988. Such prepayments are further debtors, and any amounts received in advance are creditors. In this way accountants seek to match the income relating to a particular year with the expenses of that year which have been incurred in earning that income. It is perfectly possible to prepare a schedule of any such necessary adjustments to the raw figures shown in the trial balance as shown in (1) in Appendix 2, and working from these two documents to prepare the final accounts. A better method, however, and one which makes it easier to discover and correct any arithmetical errors which might arise in the process, is to prepare an extended trial balance. To do this we use a sheet of analysis paper, and we then utilise the first two columns on the left hand side as the debit and credit columns of our raw trial balance. The reader should now turn to item 2 of Appendix 2 where this process has been carried out and the trial balance in item 1 is reproduced in this way in the appropriate columns in item 2. We then leave a space of one or two columns, and we then utilise two further columns for creditors and debtors. Note here that the creditors are shown on the left or debit column and the debtors in the right or credit column at this point. This is because as we now know every debit has a credit and vice versa. The creditors will be carried down to the credit side in the figures for next year and will be included as creditors in the balance sheet. Thus they feature as debits in this year, increasing this year's expenses or reducing this year's income items. The converse applies to the debtors.

We next have a group of four columns being a debit and a credit for Income and Expenditure Account items and a debit and a credit for Balance Sheet items on the right hand side of our sheet of analysis paper. We are now ready to calculate the figures which will be included in our final accounts. First we insert in the creditors column on the same line as the appropriate item in the trial balance, the amount of any creditor relating to the item. In our example we have a small item of £2 for insurance. The trial balance had no insurances included, we therefore make a separate line for the insurance account and insert the £2 item accordingly. Similarly, in the debtors column we insert the amounts receivable. In our example we have £50 due for subscriptions and £25.50 for dining. The next step is to add the figures across the page, and insert the resulting figures in the Income and Expenditure or Balance Sheet columns as appropriate. In our example we have £300 subscriptions in the trial balance credit column and a £50 debtor also in a credit column. We add these together and insert the answer (£350) in the credit column of the Income and Expenditure Account. Had the £50 been a creditor, it would have appeared in a debit column, and instead of adding it to the £300 credit, we would have deducted it making the result £250. At this point it is worth noting that we have shown both the debit and the credit trial balance items plus the debtor in the Income and Expenditure Account columns. This is because when we prepare the Income and Expenditure Account we wish to show both sides, that is the income and the expense. We could, of course, have netted the figures up thus £1248.01 (Dr) — £976.59 (Cr) — £25.50 (Cr) = £246.01 Dr in the Income and Expenditure Account column. This is the net cost of dining as finally shown in our Income and Expenditure Account in Appendix 3, and this treatment would be equally valid, but less informative.

In deciding whether the items go in the Income and Expenditure Account or Balance Sheet we have regard to the classification of balances indicated above. Expenses and Gains go into the Income and Expenditure Account. Assets and liabilities and capital (the accumulated fund) are balance sheet items. Losses are either expenses to be included as such, or are the net result of the summation of income and expenditure and, as in our example, are thrown up by the Income and Expenditure Account, and subsequently deducted from the Accumulated Fund or Capital (see Appendix 3).

The next step is to cast up the debtors and creditors columns and include the totals thereof in the debit and credit Balance Sheet columns respectively. Finally we add up the Income and Expenditure Account columns and strike the balances. In our case we find an excess of expenditure over income. This we insert in the credit of the Income and Expenditure columns, and carry it across to the debit Balance Sheet column. If we now cast up the balance sheet columns they should agree, as in fact in our example they do. All that now remains is to transfer the figures to the appropriate places in the final accounts.

Preparing the Final Accounts

It has been said of Accountancy that it is the science of aggregates. Without entering into the somewhat academic debate as to whether accountancy may properly be described as a science or an art, it must be said that there is a good deal of truth in this statement for the individual items in an Income and Expenditure Account or a Balance Sheet have little to tell us by themselves. They have much more to tell us if they are intelligently grouped together so as to throw up totals which will tell us how much income, or how much expense, arose from related aspects of the organisation. Accounts are in reality a report upon the financial position, and the figures should be grouped in a meaningful way. In a business, for example, it is sensible to group together all the staff costs such as salaries, national insurance and pensions to show the total costs of employment of people, or the rent, rates and repairs to premises, to show the occupancy costs of buildings. In the accounts of a lodge similar principles apply. In the example of an Income and Expenditure Account and Balance Sheet shown in Appendix 3 this principle has been adopted. The dues to Grand Lodge and Provincial Grand Lodge are grouped together, as are the costs of meetings and the general costs of administration. In the Balance Sheet the current assets are grouped, and the creditor is shown as a deduction therefrom, because the net current assets so disclosed tell us the funds currently available to run the lodge.

The figures are transferred to the respective positions assigned to them in the Income and Expenditure Account and the Balance Sheet from the details disclosed in the extended trial balance described above. It should be noted that instead of the now old fashioned two sided account once used for this purpose, the statement form of account has been adopted. In the Income and Expenditure Account, this begins by stating the items of income which are then aggregated, and then listing under the appropriate groupings properly headed, the various expenses. These are sub-totalled in their groupings, and finally the subtotals are totalled to give a total of expenses which in turn is deducted from the income total to give a final figure of net surplus or, as in our case, deficit. The surplus or deficit is added to or deducted from the opening figure of accumulated fund included in the Balance Sheet. A moments' thought will make obvious the reason for this, since if there is a surplus, the opening figure of Accumulated Fund brought forward at the beginning of the year is augmented, or, if there is a deficiency, depleted, by the results of the year's activities. In the balance sheet, the assets are grouped as 'fixed assets' or 'current assets'. The fixed assets are those which are not normally turned into cash in the course of the activities, but form part of the fixed corpus of the organisation. In a business these would be such items as plant, machinery, furniture or buildings. The current assets are those used in the day to day running of the operations. A balance sheet can therefore be considered as a statement of 'what we have less what we owe', the result being equivalent to our capital or net worth, or in our case, the Accumulated Fund.

The reader should now work carefully through the Income and Expenditure and Balance Sheet columns in the extended trial balance in Appendix 2, following the transfer of the respective items therein to the final accounts in Appendix 3. In this way it will become clear how the final accounts are constructed from the figures in the extended trial balance.

It is worth noting that in practice it is useful to show last years figures in a column next to this year's details as shown opposite (*fig 18*). This is not done in the example in Appendix 3 since the example is intended for instructional purposes, and the preceding year's figures may tend to confuse.

Closing Down the Ledger

When the final accounts have been prepared, it remains necessary to close down the Nominal Ledger for the year bringing forward the relevant balances to the beginning of the following year. When this has been done a trial balance can be taken out, and the only items remaining as balances at the beginning of the New Year will be those which were shown in the balance sheet at the end of the year just ended. The income and expense items are written off to the Income and Expenditure Account, and the Balance Sheet items are the balances carried forward. If reference is now made to the ledger following the final accounts in Appendix 3, this process will be seen to have been carried out and the ledger as shown in Appendix 2 is now closed down following the preparation of the Final Accounts. If we now take out a trial balance from this ledger, not forgetting the closing bank balance, the result will be seen to be as shown in *fig 19*.

Fig 18

Exborough Lodge No XXXX
Balance Sheet at 31st August 1987

		1987		1986
Fixed Assets				
500 Shares in Exborough Masonic Hall Ltd		500.00		500.00
Current Assets				
Debtors (Subscription & Dining Fees)	75.50		20.00	
Balance at Bank	146.53		450.00	
	222.03		470.00	
Deduct Creditor	2.00		—	
Net Current Assets		220.03		470.00
		£720.03		£970.00
Accumulated Fund				
Balance at 1st September 1986		970.00		958.50
Deduct: Excess of Expenditure for the year (1986 surplus)		249.97		11.50
		£720.03		£970.00

Fig 19

Closing Trial Balance

NL						
2	Subscriptions	50	00			
3	Dining	25	50			
12	Exborough Masonic Hall Co.	500	00			
13	Accumulated Fund			720	03	
14	Insurance			2	00	
	Balance at Bank	146	53			
		722	03	722	03	

Note that as indicated above the items now remaining are the items shown in the balance sheet.

Eliminating the Nominal Ledger

In our discussion of the analysed cash book, mention was made of the possibility in the simple case of eliminating the ledger. It was there indicated, however, that the main discussion herein would proceed on the basis that a ledger was maintained, though at the appropriate stage we would see how in certain circumstances the ledger can be eliminated.

We saw above how to prepare an extended trial balance from a ledger. The form of trial balance used had eight significant cash columns. A more sophisticated version includes two further columns which can be used to transfer items from one account to another, to correct errors and make similar adjustments. These columns also are debit and credit and are used like the journal illustrated (*fig 5*), except that no narrative is used. Such a ruling is included in the further extended trial balance, item 3 in Appendix 2. This trial balance shows how we can use this form of document to eliminate the ledger.

Reference to item 3 Appendix 2 will show that the first two columns are no longer the trial balance extracted from the ledger. Instead, they are the opening trial balance from the preceding year. Were we using this method, the trial balance shown above (*fig 19*) would be the opening figure for next year. The next two columns are used to record the items taken from the analysed cash book. Note that the items appearing as totals on the credit side of this book are entered in the debit cash book column and vice versa. Note also that the total receipts after eliminating contras are entered against the bank balance in the debit column and the total payments similarly adjusted against this item in the credit column so maintaining our principles of double entry and posting across. Next come the transfer columns mentioned above, but not used in the example. The remaining columns for creditors, debtors, Income & Expenditure Account and Balance Sheet are the same as before. The extended trial balance thus produced is now extended across the page exactly as before, and gives precisely the same result as in item 2, though one or two of the entries are in different order. By this method, in the simple case the ledger can be eliminated, the balance sheet items being carried forward to the opening columns for the following year.

Audit

It has been pointed out at the beginning of this chapter that rule 153 of the *Book of Constitutions* requires the appointment of an audit committee to report to the members of the lodge. It is, perhaps, worthy of note at this point that the Master is entitled, under the provisions of rule 154 of the *Book of Constitutions* to preside over any committee of the lodge. He is therefore entitled to preside over the audit committee, though in the great majority of cases he does not in fact do so, the work being carried out by the elected auditors. We may perhaps consider this aspect of lodge affairs under two main heads, namely preparation for audit, and the work of the audit. First however it may be as well to make a few general observations upon audit. There has, over the years, been considerable debate upon the objectives of an audit, and it is now generally agreed among accountants that the principle objective of an audit is to provide independent verification of the accounts being examined. In the audit of most commercial undertakings, and in particular limited companies, the auditor expresses an opinion as to whether or not the accounts in question give 'a true and fair view' of the profit and state of affairs of the business. This term is a term of art which has acquired a special significance in the accountancy profession, requiring consideration of numerous technical questions of standard accounting practice. We shall therefore avoid the use of this expression, although doubtless many readers will be familiar with it. As has been said, the auditing profession takes the view that the principle objective of an audit is to provide independent verification, but this notion certainly differs from the public conception of an audit which envisages the intention as being very much bound up with the safeguarding and custody of assets, particularly cash and easily negotiable assets. In a large organisation it is fairly evident that the safety of the assets must be the primary concern of the management, and the auditor can often do little more than ensure that they are carrying out this duty properly. In a much smaller organisation such as a masonic lodge, the auditor can provide a much more positive assurance upon these matters and his activities can be much closer to the general idea of the average man as to what an auditor should be doing. The distinction is therefore perhaps mainly related to the size or complexity of the organisation whose accounts are being audited, and we can perhaps say with some confidence that the auditor of a masonic lodge should consider himself as charged with ensuring, so far as possible, that the accounts of the lodge fairly present its financial position, and that the assets of the lodge are intact.

Preparation for Audit

Preparation for audit may be said to be a continuing process, beginning with the treasurer's activities in collecting and paying out monies, and recording transactions. The subscription income of the lodge can be verified by comparing the contents of the Members' Register with the list of members. This will often be printed on the summons and should be easily obtainable from the Secretary. The details included in relation to dining receipts can also be verified by reference to the attendance book, and the Secretary will usually provide the treasurer with particulars as to this. These particulars should be carefully filed and available for the examination of the auditors. Charity collections at lodge meetings should be independently counted, and the treasurer or charity steward should obtain the signature of the master or secretary in confirmation of the sums collected. These vouchers should also be retained and filed in order for inspection. The minute book will often contain particulars of charity receipts and will, of course, record any changes in subscription levels. Accordingly this book should be available to the auditors. In addition the auditors will require to familiarise themselves with the by-laws of the lodge insofar as they bear upon financial matters, and the treasurer should ensure that an up to date copy thereof is available. In making payments from lodge funds the treasurer should always obtain receipts and should retain these together with relevant invoices or statements, and these should be filed in order of the payments made and produced to the audit committee. In addition the audit committee will require to see the following:

(1) The books of account and the Members Register

(2) The bank statement

(3) Paying-in books and cheque stubs

(4) Building Society books and records relating to any other accounts.

(5) Counterfoil receipts for subscriptions, etc.

The treasurer should also arrange for the bank to send a letter direct to the auditors confirming the bank balances at the accounting date, and detailing any assets (eg investments) held for safe custody. Some banks today are beginning to make a charge for such letters in commercial cases. The extent of the verification required by auditors in such cases is, however, often very extensive. It is the writer's view that such charges are difficult to justify in the case of the very much simpler requirements of a Masonic lodge.

In preparing his accounts the treasurer will have reconciled the bank (see above *fig 17*). In addition he will have listed the debtors and creditors. These documents should be produced to the audit committee to assist it in the task of verification.

The work of the Audit

We have seen that the auditors' duty is to ensure that the accounts fairly present the financial position, and that the assets of the lodge are intact. To do this they must verify the income and expenditure by vouching it against the documentation provided by the treasurer as indicated above and taking care that the invoices relate to the lodge and are proper to it. The extent of that verification is a matter for the judgement of the auditors themselves, but it must be stressed that they must do sufficient work for them to be able to feel fully satisfied that their duties have been properly discharged. Thus in the smaller case they may examine every receipt and payment. In the larger case they may feel able to content themselves with testing only a proportion of some of the items. In either case, however, their overall responsibility is the same, and at the end of the day they must feel fully satisfied. They should work through the treasurer's working papers, verifying the transfer of the various items to the final accounts. Any assets of the lodge will be reflected in the balance sheet, and their examination of the documentation will enable them to verify the figures. The certificates from the bank will provide evidence of the existence of those assets in the bank's custody. If there are stocks, for example of publications, lists should be produced and checked by the audit committee. Lodge equipment will usually be written off at the time of purchase. This will often not be in the custody of the treasurer and except when purchased may not reflect in the lodge accounts. The audit committee should nevertheless enquire into this matter and ensure that such equipment is kept in safe custody. There should rarely be cash in hand. If however there is such cash, the relevant accounts should be vouched up to date and the cash counted.

The Audit Report

We have seen that the *Book of Constitutions* requires the auditors to report upon the financial position of the lodge, and to check all balances. We have also seen that in certain respects this rule must today be considered somewhat out of date and not in accordance with modern audit thought. The report should, however, be framed with the rule in mind, and the following is a suggested report to be made where the audit has, as in the vast majority of cases, been satisfactory:

Report of the Auditors to the Members of Exborough Lodge No. XXXX

I/We have audited the accounts of the lodge for the Year ended 31st August 1987 in accordance with the requirements of Rule 153 of the Book of Constitutions. In my/our opinion the accounts fairly present the excess of income (expenditure) over expenditure(income) for the year and the financial position of the lodge at that date. I/We have verified the balances held by the lodge at the 31st August 1987 in accordance with the said Rule 153.

Date .... Signed...................

48

In any case where a clear report upon the above lines cannot be given, the reasons for qualifying the report should be clearly stated.

The above report may, of course, be used with appropriate modification in connection with any funds not held by the treasurer, for example charity funds held by the Charity Steward, and subject to audit in the same way.

Chapter 5

Masonic Halls & Trading Activities

IN THIS CHAPTER it is intended to consider the position of those lodges which own their own halls, and perhaps operate a bar or some other activity of a similar kind such as catering. Many masonic halls are owned by small private companies whose capital has been subscribed by the lodges which make use of the hall and its facilities. The activities and accounting of such companies are beyond the scope of this book. They are governed by the requirements of company law, and will employ the services of professional accountants in the role of auditors. It will be their function to give guidance to such companies. There are, however, many cases where a lodge has raised funds to acquire its own property, or where a generous brother in the past has donated a hall or left funds for its construction. In these cases the hall is not owned by a company but directly by the lodge, and it is cases of this nature with which we are here concerned.

Trustees

A masonic lodge is in reality a specialised form of unincorporated members' club. As such, its assets belong to the members for the time being, but in English law a property cannot be directly owned by a greater number of individuals than four. For this reason, freehold property owned by a lodge is usually registered in the names of trustees and they hold the property for the benefit of all the members for the time being. Trustees are, of course, appointed from time to time by the lodge for this purpose and the office is often seen as having some special significance. In reality, however, it is no more than a legal convenience. In many cases of this nature the lodge will go further and charge the trustees with the duty of managing the property. In such cases the legal position as to ownership is unchanged and the additional duties imposed upon the trustees are no more than a request to the trustees to undertake these duties. Trustees who accept this obligation are of course answerable to the lodge for their actions, but not as a general requirement of the law of property, only as an additional responsibility which they have agreed to accept. A lodge may, of course, have raised money and formed a specific trust under deed and trustees may be appointed under this trust. In this case their duties will be regulated by the deed of trust, and their duty of management may flow from this source.

Where a lodge in this position uses the property only for its own meetings no particular problems arise. The expenses of maintaining and managing the property will fall upon the lodge and will be a proper charge in its accounts. The subscriptions paid by the members will require to be sufficient for these purposes, and care will require to be taken to set them at such a level as to ensure that funds are available for such expenses as redecoration and the occasional heavy repair bill which might arise. Many of the properties concerned are old, and these costs can be considerable. In such cases all the costs of managing and maintaining the property should be grouped together in the Income and Expenditure Account so that it can be clearly seen by the members, and they can appreciate how much of the subscription income has to be applied to these purposes.

Receipt of Rents

In such cases, however, it is much more usual for the property to be used not only by the proprietor lodge, but by other masonic organisations as well, and in these circumstances a rent is often paid by these organisations to the proprietor lodge. This can give rise to serious problems, for rents received are chargeable to tax under the relevant provisions of the taxing statutes. This aspect of the matter will be considered more fully under the chapter dealing with taxation matters, but we can note here that losses on rental income cannot be carried back against surpluses of an earlier year. They can, of course, be carried forward, but by then the damage is done, for in managing such property it is usually necessary to set rents at a level which will provide initial surpluses so that when the actual expense of maintenance arises, the funds are available to meet it. Thus the surplus arises first, and the possible deficiency later. Tax is then payable on the surplus, and the subsequent deficiency is only available against future surpluses. This process has a tendency to repeat itself, so that unless steps are taken to mitigate the impact of the taxing statutes, over the years considerable sums can become payable to the Inland Revenue. In passing it may perhaps be appropriate to observe that rent of this nature has no VAT consequences because land is exempt from VAT.

Catering Activities

There is a further difficulty which must be considered. A lodge such as we are considering, having its own hall, may well equip this with a bar. There will, moreover, usually be catering arrangements. Provided they are confined to the lodge there are likely to be no Corporation Tax consequences, and the turnover is unlikely to reach levels which could give rise to a necessity to register for VAT. If, however, the Masonic Hall Trustees acting on behalf of the lodge, let the hall to other masonic organisations, and in addition managed the bar and the catering, the lodge would be trading, and the profits arising from this activity would be chargeable to Corporation Tax. Even if these activities were franchised to a caterer, the profits accruing to the lodge perhaps on a percentage basis, or something of this sort, would be chargeable. Moreover, in such a case the level of activity could well rise to the point where the lodge became registerable for VAT. The consequences of this could be disastrous, for if the lodge were so registered, VAT would become chargeable not only on the catering activities but on the subscriptions also, and even leaving this aside, the financial consequences would be quite unacceptable. Of course, the bar and catering activities might well be left to the individual bodies using the hall, and if each independently made its own arrangements the tax consequences of catering might well not arise, but the rental problem would remain.

Separation of Lodges from Quasi Commercial Activities

In these circumstances it is clear that for the individual lodge to manage a hall and let the hall to other bodies, whether with catering or otherwise, can be very unsatisfactory and some other solution must be found. The taxation principle of mutuality is discussed more fully in chapter 8 on Taxation, but here it can be said that the profits of mutual activity are not chargeable to Income Tax or Corporation Tax, thus if a mutual organisation can be devised to operate the hall, this problem can be eliminated. The VAT problem will remain, but this will affect the mutual organisation and not the lodge itself. Thus the first thing that emerges from this is the proposition that in cases such as we are considering, the hall and its management are much better hived off from the lodge itself. This does not mean that the lodge need divest itself of its freehold, but that it would be wise to set up a separate organisation to look after this interest. There are a number of ways in which this can be one. Various possibilities are discussed below:-

1. *Limited Company*

It is possible to set up a limited company to take over the management of the hall, with or without responsibility for catering. In such a case the lodge would let the hall to the company at a peppercorn rent, and the company would take over all the quasi commercial activities. The possible share structures are almost infinitely variable. For example the lodge could own all the shares itself with the consequence that any return on the shares would go to lodge funds. Dividends are taxed at source, so that if in receipt of these, the lodge would have borne income tax. It is itself liable to Corporation Tax, but effectively there would, in the present state of the law, be no further liability. Alternatively the lodge could constitute its Benevolent Fund a charity (see chapter 7) in which case it could arrange for shares to be held by the charity which would reclaim any tax deducted. It could also arrange for the company to covenant its income to the charity with similar results.

Alternatively the lodge could give the other bodies using the hall the opportunity to subscribe for shares and they could if they so wished, arrange their affairs in like manner.

2. *Limited Company with Club*

A company could be organised as above with the catering activities hived off to a club. The club members would be the lodges and lodge members concerned, and all catering profits would be mutual profits and not liable to Income or Corporation Tax.

3. *Masonic Mutual Society*

Where rent only was involved, the lodge could organise a mutual organisation to which all lodges and their members using the hall would belong. The hall would be let to this organisation for a peppercorn rent, and it would be responsible for the management of the hall on behalf of the member lodges. Any income would thus be mutual income and not chargeable to Income or Corporation Tax. VAT would not arise because land is exempt from charge.

4. *Masonic Club*

A masonic club, is, of course, merely a form of mutual society. The club would take a lease of the hall at a peppercorn rent and would then be responsible for all rental maintenance and catering. All the lodges, and thus members using the hall, would be members of the Masonic Club, and all income arising from their mutual activities would be exempt from Income and Corporation Tax.

It should be noted that in all the above cases (except 3 as indicated) VAT could arise, but this would not be the responsibility of the proprietor lodge. It would, of course, be for the individual lodge to consider which of the above plans, or some variant thereof would best suit its individual circumstances. Of one thing, however, one can be certain. Any of these plans is preferable to the dangers of exposing the lodge itself to the rigours of Corporation Tax and VAT.

Chapter 6

Budgets:

General Considerations

THE PREPARATION OF simple budgets is an essential part of the duties of a Masonic treasurer, since as we have seen the treasurer's responsibility extends beyond the care of the assets entrusted to him, to the necessity to ensure that when expenses arise the funds are available to meet them. In a commercial organisation the preparation of budgets, and their use as a means of controlling the commercial operations, can be a complex matter; but in the small lodge or indeed other society, the complexities are very greatly reduced. Some, however, of the same principles require to be applied. Budgetting in the small voluntary society begins with a consideration of the expenses to be met and their nature. Expenses are divisible into fixed, semi-variable and variable expenses. The fixed expenses are those which will arise whatever the level of activity. In a masonic lodge there would be such matters as for example Tyler fees. Sometimes temple hire is a fixed charge being in the nature of rent. In some other cases it may vary according to the numbers in the lodge on a per capita basis as indeed will dues to Grand Lodge and Province. The costs of dining in some lodges are included in the annual subscription, and where this is so, the subscription will need to be fixed at a level sufficient to pay, not only the due proportion of fixed expenses, but also the average cost of meals for all the meetings in the year. Due to the impact of inflation in recent years, the costs of meals have tended to rise year by year and this has caused a considerable problem, in that lodges in this position have found it necessary to revise their byelaws every year or two. This has caused the Grand Lodge to relax the rules concerning subscriptions in this respect, and lodges are now encouraged to adopt a form of byelaws which enables them to vary the dining charge by resolution without a change of byelaws. The necessity to budget extends, of course, to those lodges which operate Masonic Halls, and estimates will be necessary in respect of lighting and heating costs, the cost of preparing meals and the like. In such cases rates, for example, would be a fixed cost, but lighting and heating may be variable or semi-variable, being dependent on the number of meetings held. The expenses of such institutions will, of course, cover a wider range than those for the lodge which rents accommodation.

The Lodge Budget in Practice

With a new lodge care will need to be taken to ensure that all the likely expenses are included in the initial budget, and the matter will no doubt be discussed very fully by the committee before the consecration of the lodge.

With the ongoing lodge, the treasurer will have available to him the Income and Expenditure Account of the previous year. As we have seen, the Exborough Lodge in our example in Appendix 2 made a deficit in the year 1986/87 of £249.97. Clearly this cannot be allowed to continue, and we can see that all but about £4.00 of this deficit is the result of an excess of dining costs. The lodge is, of course, one which has taken advantage of the right to vary its dining charges by resolution, but no doubt it incurs certain dining costs as expenses of the lodge. These are, for example, meals for the Tyler, and doubtless at the installation meeting there are guests of the lodge to be paid for. Moreover the result achieved has been struck after including in the income initiation fees. It is recommended that an attempt be made to balance income and expenditure without taking initiation fees into account. These can be set aside to meet the registration fees and any other initiation costs, and any surplus can be added to the lodge funds. This is particularly advisable in cases were the subscription does not include dining. In the other case, where dining is included, there will be some absentees, and the lack of necessity to pay for their dining will in such cases give a buoyancy to the revenue which in the present case will not be present. Bearing these factors in mind, it is evident that the difficulties of the Exborough Lodge do not merely arise from a failure to budget sufficiently for dining costs. The subscription has been insufficient to cover other charges. The lodge is, of course, very small, and this factor bears heavily upon it.

Fig 20

EXBOROUGH LODGE   BUDGET 1987/88

		Item	Expenses 1986/87	Estimated Expenses 1987/88	
Dues	Grand Lodge	1	92 00	Dues for 15 members+VAT+Year Book	103 28
	Provincial Grand Lodge	2	46 00	Dues for 15 members+VAT+Year Book	47 12
Meeting	Dining	3	246 00	5 meals for Tyler, 2 masters guests) 2 lodge guests, 2 installation guests) 11 lodge guests at say 12.50)	137 50
	Temple Hire	4	93 00	5 meetings at £20	100 00
	Tyler	5	40 00	5 meetings at £10	50 00
Administration	Printing Stationery & Postage	6	50 00	Allow 10% increase	55 00
	Insurance	7	2 00	No change	2 00
	Committee Rooms	8	15 00	3 meetings at £6	18 00
	Subscription	9	8 00	No change	8 00
	Regalia	10	43 00	Allow 5% increase	45 00
	Rituals	11	25 00	Small stock held – annual cost say	8 00
			£660 00		£623 90

Number of members 15 therefore
Subscription £624/15=£41.60 say £42.00

If we now turn to *fig 20* we can see the budget for the year 1987/88. The treasurer has a very difficult task, for although the total costs are lower for 1987/88 this is due to the fact that the net cost of dining has been carefully budgeted to restrict it to lodge guests. In the previous year it is evident that the costs were not fully recovered from members. Assuming that the dining costs include wines, the treasurer must recommend a dining fee of £12 for installation nights, and perhaps a little less, say £11.50 for other evenings. Alternatively he may suggest that wines be excluded and left to the individual member. In the budget, the guests and Tyler have been budgeted a little on the high side. Last year 95 meals cost an average of £13, but it is assumed that this included an unusually high number of guests of the lodge. Examination of the caterer's charges is assumed to indicate that the above figures can be attained, but the Secretary would need to be warned of the need to keep dining costs down. In addition, since the budget must be met from the fifteen members, the subscription would need to be £624/15 = £41.60, or say £42. If, of course, it is intended to initiate a new brother there will, in addition be an initiation fee less the dues, and this should produce about £50 net. Part of this could be used to reduce the burden on members, but as indicated above, this course of action is not recommended.

It will be noted that the various items in the budget in *fig 20* are annotated, and allowance has been made for a number of increases in expenses. Some of these cannot be controlled. For example item 4, temple hire, is a fixed cost, and the charge has been increased from £18.50 to £20. Similarly item 5, the Tyler's fee shows an increase which is probably unavoidable. Committee rooms (item 8) is also increased. This, however, might be reduced or even eliminated if a brother could be persuaded to allow his home to be used for this purpose. Printing too can sometimes be reduced greatly by use of modern copying machines. The treasurer should explore every avenue to contain the expenses as far as possible. In many lodges, of course, the problems will be less acute, but the example given here is chosen to illustrate in a succinct manner the nature of the treasurer's task, and the methods necessary to discharge it.

Chapter 7

Charitable Monies

General Considerations

Charitable activity is a major part of the work of a Masonic Lodge, and the collection of funds for charitable purposes will always be a matter of great importance to the brethren. The task of organising the charitable collections within each lodge is the responsibility of the Charity Steward, though in most cases care of the funds in question will be an additional responsibility falling upon the treasurer. This is not always so, of course. In some lodges the Charity Steward will himself have this responsibility. Whatever may be the position in this respect, however, the principles to be followed in relation to charitable monies will be no different.

Charitable monies should never on any account be retained in the same bank or other account as general lodge funds. Separate accounts should always be opened and strict attention should be paid to the necessity to keep charitable monies in these separate accounts. Failure to follow this principle could very easily lead to the position where at some point the lodge would itself be overdrawn, and might therefore be effectively subsidising its ordinary activities with funds earmarked for charitable purposes. Certainly there would never be any intention to do this, but were the monies not kept entirely separate, the fact could easily be inadvertently overlooked, and would no doubt appear to correct itself when the next tranche of subscriptions or other general monies was received.

The Benevolent Funds of most masonic lodges are usually very simple in nature, and will not normally involve assets beyond cash held in bank and building society accounts. Such funds, although often informal in their structure, probably fall within the well established definitions of charitable funds. This question of what constitutes a charity is not the recent creation

of the Charity Commission. It originally derives from the old Poor Law
and has been defined as:–

(1) Trusts for the relief of poverty

(2) Trusts for the benefit of education

(3) Trusts for the furtherance of religion

(4) Trusts established for any other purpose analogous thereto.

Clearly the average lodge benevolent fund is likely to be well within this
definition, whether a registered charity or not. A charity is required to be
registered with the Charity Commission, however, in any case where it
holds property, or investments to the value of £15 or more. Thus a lodge
benevolent fund holding investments may well be registrable and this
possibility should not be overlooked.

The Charitable Income

The income of most lodge benevolent funds will normally consist of the
following:

(1) Charity collections

(2) Receipts from raffles and social occasions

(3) Donations from lodge general funds or from members

(4) Interest received

From the totality of the monies collected expenditure would normally
consist of annual donations to one or other of the Masonic Charities,
donations to the W. Master's list for charitable purposes, donations to local
charities, and benevolence to brethren, widows, children and others in need
of assistance.

It is here worth noting that payments to the Fund of Benevolence under
rules 269 and 271 of the *Book of Constitutions* may be made from the

benevolent fund, though it is only proper to point out that it is understood that it would be the hope of Grand Lodge that lodges endeavour to meet this obligation from general funds. Nevertheless we may note that had the Exborough Lodge taken the course of meeting its rule 271 contribution from benevolent funds its budgeted subscription might have been reduced accordingly (see *fig 20*).

In cases of the nature under consideration where the balance of available funds is held in bank or similar accounts, as indicated above, nothing more than a simple Receipts and Payments Account is required. A balance sheet would be useful only in circumstances where there were substantial other assets such as investments.

Books and Accounts

The record keeping for the simple benevolent fund need be no more than the simple cash book illustrated in Chapter 3 (*fig 8*). An analysed cash book would normally be quite unnecessary for this simple purpose, it being a very easy matter to analyse the receipts and payments at the end of each year.

An alternative form of cash book which may be found useful for this purpose is the three columned cash book, which enables a check to be kept on the running balance of charitable monies. Such a book would be as illustrated below:−

Fig 21

1987			Dr	Cr	Balance
Jan 1	Balance	b/f	100 00		100 00
14	Collections-festive Bd		25 00		125 00
31	Exborough Hospice			50 00	75 00

A typical Receipts and Payments Account for a lodge benevolent fund is as illustrated in *fig 22*. As we have seen, in such a case a balance sheet would be

Fig 22

EXBOROUGH LODGE NO. XXXX
BENEVOLENT FUND
FOR THE YEAR ENDED 31ST AUGUST 1987

	1987		1986	
Accumulated Fund at 1st September 1986		840 00		622 88
Add: Receipts for the Year ended 31st August 1987				
Charity Collections	137 50		127 00	
Raffles, etc	205 00		185 50	
Donations from Lodge Funds	50 00		50 00	
Interest—Bank Deposit Account	27 35		24 22	
Exborough Building Society	44 20		42 40	
Total Receipts		464 05		429 12
		1304 05		1052 00
Less: Payments for the Year ended 31st August 1987				
Provincial Festival	100 00		50 00	
RMBI—Masters list	100 00		100 00	
Exborough Hospice	50 00		50 00	
Exborough Hospital Scanner Appeal	50 00		—	
Flowers & Local Benevolence	15 00		12 00	
Total Payments		315 00		212 00
Accumulated Fund at 31st August 1987		£989 05		£840 00
Represented by: Deposit Account—Universal Bank plc		389 05		240 00
Deposit Account—Exborough Building Society		600 00		600 00
		£989 05		£840 00

quite unnecessary. In the more complex case when a balance sheet was needed, the method of preparing it would be no different from the methods already discussed. It should, however, be noted that adjustments to a simple charity account for payments in advance or accruals due would usually be inappropriate. Different considerations might arise in the case of a larger charitable fund where there were expenses of administration and the like, but we are not here concerned with such funds.

There are, of course, some cases in which a lodge benevolent fund has benefitted from the gift, or bequest of some generous brother. In these cases, the gift in question may be made upon specific conditions. For example a legacy may be left on the basis that the funds are invested and the income used for a specified class of benevolence. In such circumstances, a balance sheet would be essential.

Such funds would normally require to be kept separately from general benevolent funds and accounts would need to reflect the position. In such a case the benevolent fund would almost certainly be registrable, and the treasurer may need to seek expert guidance. In this connection attention is drawn not only to the accounting aspects of the matter, but also to the observations on the matter of investment in Chapter 2. In the vast majority of cases, however, no such problems are likely to arise, and the foregoing suggestions will be found to be perfectly adequate in accounting for benevolent funds.

Charitable Trusts and Covenanted Payments

Payment to charitable institutions under deed of covenant is a familiar device, and most readers will be familiar with such schemes even if they do not fully understand the mechanism by which they operate. To understand this matter it is necessary to bear in mind the fact that a charity is exempt from taxation on income from interest, annuities, dividends and rents. A charity is not exempt in respect of income from trade except in certain very limited circumstances, but this aspect of the matter is beyond the scope of this work, and need not concern us here.

Dividends in the United Kingdom are paid effectively under deduction of income tax, for a tax credit is given with each dividend paid by a UK company equivalent to income tax at the current basic rate on an amount equal to the dividend received plus the tax credit so given. A charity in receipt of such dividends is entitled to make a claim on the Inland Revenue to recover the amount of such tax credits. A payment under a deed of covenant is an annual payment, or a form of annuity. The person making the payment is required to deduct tax therefrom at the basic rate, and this tax too, if the payment is made to a charity, may be recovered by the charity. The payer of the covenant enters particulars on his tax return, but since in calculating his tax payable at the basic rate, he is not entitled to deduct the amount of the covenant from his gross income, he effectively pays over to the Inland Revenue the tax which he has deducted from the payment under covenant. The following may serve to illustrate the effects of the transactions:

Fig 23

	£		Tax £	Net Income £		£
Gross Income	10000	@ 27%	2700	7300		
Covenanted Payment	100	Retained	(27)	27	Paid to charity	83
Income Net of Covenant	£9900	@ 27%	£2673	£7327		
					Charity Reclaims	27
					Received by charity	£100

In addition to the above, the higher rate taxpayer is now entitled to deduct the gross amount of such covenanted payments from his total taxable income so reducing the amount upon which higher rate tax is paid by the amount of such covenanted payments.

This system is operated by all the major Masonic charities, and indeed by most, or perhaps all the major charities in this country. It is also operated by many minor charities, by churches and the like. There is indeed no reason whatever why a masonic lodge should not formalise its own benevolent fund by creating a charitable trust. In this way it could greatly increase the amount of charitable money available. If, for example, the brethren could be persuaded to enter into small deeds of covenant to cover charitable collections in lodge or at the festive board, for every £100 collected the benevolent fund could recover from the Inland Revenue a further £32–53 at current rates of income tax. It is stressed, however, that if such a plan is adopted, it must be run conscientiously and with care. It is quite useless to enter upon this course and subsequently fail to deal properly with the scheme.

The Charitable Trust

Having described the system of payments under deed of covenant, and indicated that in suitable circumstances a Masonic lodge could itself operate such a scheme, it is proposed to indicate how a scheme of this nature could be established and managed. The first step would be the establishment of a charitable trust, and in this connection the lodge would require formally to resolve that such a trust be established and certain brethren be authorised to execute the appropriate trust deed. Probably the Worshipful Master, Treasurer and Secretary would be charged with this task. A specimen trust deed is illustrated in Appendix 4. Consideration would then require to be given to whether or not the new charity should be registered (see above).

The next step would be to persuade as many brethren as possible to enter into deeds of covenant to cover lodge charity collections. In this connection it should be noted that legislation has now reduced the term for valid deeds of covenant from seven years to four years. A suitable form of deed of covenant is also illustrated in Appendix 4. Arrangements should then be made for brethren who had entered into deeds of covenant to pay their charitable collections to the Charity Steward in small envelopes. The style of envelope in question will be familiar to most readers. It will be necessary to keep a register of covenanted income received. A suitable form of register covering four years with five meetings each year is illustrated in Appendix 4. It will be noted that space is provided for the following particulars.

(1) The number of the Deed of Covenant

(2) The name of the covenantor

(3) The net annual sum covenanted (this is the sum to be collected)

(4) A space for each of five meetings a year for four years.

All the above is fairly self-explanatory. The details in 4, namely the number of meetings each year would depend upon the number of meetings of the lodge held each year. More than four years would be recorded, of course, merely by continuing overleaf. The deeds of covenant would be carefully filed in order of the register, and as each deed lapsed by effluxion of time, the brother concerned could be approached to renew it. If a brother were absent from a meeting, his contribution would nevertheless be collected as soon as convenient. Brethren would then be required to complete the appropriate revenue form R185 to enable the repayment to be claimed, and after the 5th April each year a claim for repayment would need to be submitted to the Inland Revenue Claims Branch, Charity Division, Magdalen House, Trinity Road, Bootle, Merseyside L69 9BB, which is the branch charged with dealing with charitable claims.

Chapter 8

Taxation

IN CONSIDERING THE matter of taxation in respect of a masonic lodge we have to consider Income Tax, Corporation Tax and Capital Gains Tax. We also have to deal with Value Added Tax. A masonic lodge is in fact liable to Corporation Tax in respect of any income which it might have within the charge to tax, but since Corporation Tax is based upon the rules relating to Income Tax, it is first necessary to have regard to that tax.

Income Tax—General

Income tax is a charge levied upon income from all sources. United Kingdom Income Tax regards Income as falling within six Cases and Six Schedules, with special rules relating to each Case and each Schedule. Mention is here made of this because it is important to understand that, in a general sense, these various sources of income stand alone. With certain important exceptions, mainly related to Schedule D, losses relating to one source cannot be used to offset gains from another source. We shall here be concerned with tax under Schedule A, and under Schedule D Cases I and III & VI. Schedule A is the Schedule relating to income from property, namely rents, and it is this Schedule, therefore, which has effect in relation to rents receivable in respect of letting Masonic Halls.

Schedule A: Tax is chargeable under Schedule A on the following:
   (a) Rents under leases
   (b) Rent charges, ground annuals and feu duties, and other annual payments arising from land
   (c) Other receipts arising by virtue of the ownership of land.

Tax is chargeable on the full amount of the receipts after deducting only the following:

(a) The cost of maintenance repairs insurance and management of the property

(b) The cost of services which are required to be provided where there is no separate consideration

(c) Rates and similar charges

(d) Rents, etc, payable.

It should be noted that an excess of expenditure for a previous period can be carried forward, but cannot be carried back against an earlier period. It is important to note that capital expenditure, for example, upon improvements cannot be deducted. Thus if rents are set at a level sufficient to finance future development, the surpluses arising will be taxable without future relief.

Schedule D—Case I

This Case is the trading Case, and tax is chargeable thereunder on the full amount of profits or gains arising from the carrying on of a trade. There can be no doubt that catering operations and the managing of a bar are trading operations, so that where a Masonic Lodge owns a Hall and itself carries on this type of operation, the profits are chargeable under this Schedule. Under this Case losses can be set off against other income of the year arising from all other schedules and cases.

Schedule D—Case III

This Case brings into charge to income tax all income arising from untaxed interest. The case is of less importance since bank interest became subject to charge levied on the bank at a composite rate as in the case of building societies. It is, however, still of some importance because for the purposes of computing Corporation Tax it is required to be included in the Corporation Tax Computation, and credit is then given against any liability for the amount of the addition to tax, thus:

Building Society, etc, interest received	£ 73
Grossed up for tax @ 27%	£ 27
Chargeable to Corporation Tax	£100
Corporation Tax @ 27%	£ 27
Less: Credit for grossing up factor	£ 27
Nil	NIL

The problem arises only where the rate of Corporation Tax is higher than the grossing up factor, but the fact should be borne in mind.

The main problem arises in respect of any other interest, for example from certain government stocks, which might be received. In such a Case a tax liability arises without any offset. For this reason many lodges have taken steps to ensure that interest of any sort is payable to the lodge benevolent fund. The Inland Revenue does not in practice seek to pursue such small amounts of interest accruing to such funds on the basis that they may be regarded as charitable funds. Such an arrangement is therefore to be recommended where a lodge is entitled to receive interest.

Schedule D—Case VI

This Case is the so-called 'sweeping case'. It charges to tax any annual profits or gains not otherwise chargeable. It is of importance in connection with present considerations only insofar as it covers lettings where the tenant is entitled to use furniture, and some lodges letting masonic premises have income of this nature. The rules of computation are similar to those applicable to Case I above, but unlike Case I, losses are not available against other income.

Corporation Tax

Corporation Tax is chargeable upon any body corporate or unincorporated association with the exception of partnerships, local authorities or local authority associations. A masonic lodge is therefore within the charge to Corporation Tax on any taxable income which it may have. As we have already indicated, Corporation Tax is based upon the rules of Income Tax, and it is for this reason that we have considered above the detailed Income Tax rules which are likely to be applicable to the income which lodges might be expected to enjoy.

Income Tax is charged in relation to fiscal years beginning with the 6th April annually and ending on the following 5th April, and all income charged to income tax is related to such fiscal years. Moreover, trading income for income tax purposes, in the normal year, is assessed upon the basis of the results of the financial year ended within the previous fiscal year. Similar provisions relate to Case III Interest. Under the Corporation Tax rules no such complications exist. The company (this term is used henceforth to describe all bodies within the charge to Corporation Tax) concerned is required to compute the income arising to it in its own financial year (or other period), and this income is assessed on the basis of the totality of that income for the year. The company's year is called its Chargeable Accounting Period and the tax chargeable on the basis of the period is normally assessed and payable nine months after the end of the period. For the purposes of charging tax, the Corporation Tax year is deemed to end on the 31st March annually, and the 1st April each year begins a new Corporation Tax financial year. The year from the 1st April 1987 to 31st March 1988, for example, would be called 'the Financial Year 1987'. The sole object of this is to deal with rates of tax. If a company's chargeable accounting period overlaps two Corporation Tax financial years where the rates of tax have changed, the company's chargeable profits require to be apportioned to these two years and the tax charge calculated accordingly.

The Principle of Mutuality

We referred in Chapter 5 to the principle of mutuality when discussing the taxation position of those Lodges which may own and operate a masonic hall. We have seen above, the far reaching nature of the tax charge upon various sorts of income, and it may well be asked how it is that a masonic lodge, or indeed any other similar institution is not liable to tax upon income received by way of subscriptions and the like? There will be those who answer this question by reference to the old adage that a man cannot make a profit from trading with himself. This however is not strictly the case. A very well known (to the expert) tax case established in 1955 that it is possible to make a profit from one's own activities. The principle which protects such organisations as masonic lodges from the charge to Corporation Tax is the principle of mutuality. A long line of tax cases beginning in the nineteenth century established the principle of the exemption of mutual profits from taxation as not being the result of trading. There has since been legislation bringing much mutual trading activity within the charge to Corporation Tax, but it still remains the case that a club or similar institution cannot make a taxable profit from trading with its members. It is this fact which takes the masonic lodge outside the tax net in respect of subscriptions and other similar receipts including its own lodge catering profits which might otherwise fall within the net of Case I of Schedule D. It is, moreover, this principle which should be utilised where possible by masonic organisations to ensure that as far as possible their income, such as rents, comes from the members themselves as part of a mutual organisation and as such is outside the scope of income taxation.

Capital Gains Tax

Capital Gains Tax is chargeable upon any disposal of assets. For this purpose, the main property with which a masonic lodge is likely to be concerned is freehold or leasehold property and securities. Chattels are also within the charge to Capital Gains Tax, but the gains on chattels are exempt from charge if the consideration received for each chattel does not exceed £3000, so that the likelihood of a tax charge for a lodge on this account would be very small. It must, however, be borne in mind that a lodge is chargeable to Capital Gains Tax on the disposal of securities, on the difference between the cost (including expenses) and the sale price (after deducting expenses). The sale of property gives rise to charge similarly computed. In the case of short leases, ie leases having less than 50 years to run, which are sold, the provisions are more complex and expert advice should be sought. It is thought, however, that short leases are unlikely to be of concern to many lodges.

Since 1982 a small relief from Capital Gains Tax by way of indexation against inflation has been available. Upon any disposal to which a Capital Gains Tax Charge arises, the treasurer should be aware of the existence of this relief and should ensure that in raising an assessment the Inland Revenue takes due account thereof.

Value Added Tax

VAT is a tax on the supply of goods and services in the course of business. The term business is extended to include clubs which trade with their members. Masonic Lodges are within the charge to VAT, if they have a turnover sufficient to bring them within the net. Fortunately land is exempt from charge to VAT so that those lodges which receive rent from Masonic Halls are not chargeable on this account. Mutual trading, however, is not exempt from VAT so that it is of the utmost importance that where there is a catering activity of sufficient size, it is carried on independently of the lodge. The Finance Act 1987 raised the limit for VAT registration to a turnover of £21 300 annually, or £7250 in any quarter. Lodge subscriptions, of course, do not amount to anything approaching these figures, but self-catering activities can very easily give rise to turnover of this order, and indeed far greater, so that care must be taken to ensure that the lodge is not placed in difficulties on this account. Were a lodge so unfortunate, or perhaps so foolish in the management of its affairs, as to overlook this matter, VAT would be chargeable not only in respect of the quasi-trading activities, but also in respect of all lodge dues, and indeed brethren will be familiar with the charge for VAT which is made in respect of Grand Lodge and Provincial Grand Lodge dues. These matters are therefore of some importance and should not be overlooked.

Duty to Inform Tax Authorities

It should be noted that it is the duty of the taxpayer in all the cases of taxation considered above to inform the relevant authority if he comes within the charge to tax. It is not for the Inland Revenue or Customs and Excise to enquire. Failure to report chargeability is normally a tax offence, and the treasurer must therefore regard it as his duty to ensure that the requirements of the taxing statutes as they may affect his lodge, are observed. The Finance Act is subject to change annually and the VAT registration limit is likely to be altered so lodges should make themselves aware of the latest information.

APPENDIX 1

Exborough Lodge MEMBERS REGISTER 1986/87

1986/87

|←———————— Dining ————————→|

	Arrears Brought Forward		Current Year Subs Etc		September		November		January		March		May	
		Pd		Pd		Pd		Pd		Pd		Pd		Pd
A. Abel			25 00	10/9	8 50	10/9	8 50	12/11	17 00	14/1	27 00	15/3	8 50	12/5
B. Baker			25 00	5/9	17 00	18/11	8 50	12/11	8 50	14/1	18 00	15/3	8 50	12/5
C. Charley			25 00	12/11	8 50	10/9	17 00	12/11	8 50	14/1	18 00	15/3	8 50	12/5
D. Desmond			25 00	5/9	25 50	17/9	8 50	12/11	8 50	14/1	9 00	15/3	17 00	12/5
E. Eagle			25 00	10/9	8 50	10/9	8 50	12/11	8 50	14/1	18 00	15/3	8 50	12/5
F. Forsyth			25 00	10/9	17 00	10/9	17 00	12/11	8 50	14/1	9 00	15/3	17 00	12/5
G. Gordon			25 00	17/9	8 50	17/9	17 00	12/11	17 00	14/1	45 00	15/3	8 50	12/5
H. Henry	20 00	10/9	25 00	o/s	17 00	10/9	8 50	12/11	8 50	14/1	27 00	15/3	8 50	12/5
J. Jones			Secretary		8 50	10/9	8 50	12/11	8 50	14/1	18 00	15/3	8 50	12/5
K. King			25 00	12/11	8 50	17/9	25 50	12/11	8 50	14/1	27 00	15/3	17 00	o/s
L. Love			25 00	o/s	8 50	12/11	17 00	12/11	17 00	14/1	9 00	15/3	8 50	12/5
M. Merry			25 00	10/9	8 50	10/9	8 50	12/11	8 50	14/1	9 00	15/3	17 00	12/5
N. Newman			25 00	17/9	8 50	10/9	8 50	12/11	17 00	14/1	18 00	15/3	17 00	12/5
P. Peters			25 00	10/9	8 50	10/9	8 50	12/11	8 50	14/1	27 00	15/3	8 50	o/s
R. Rogers		Initiation	60 00	10/9										
		Subscription	25 00	10/9	25 50	10/9	8 50	12/11	8 50	14/1	9 00	15/3	25 50	12/5
Total Due	20 00		410 00		187 00		178 50		161 50		288 00		187 00	
Unpaid at Year End			50 00										25 50	
Collected	20 00		360 00		187 00		178 50		161 50		288 00		161 50	

Subscription Paid	300 00
Initiation Paid	60 00
	360 00

Total Dining 976 50

76

1987/88

|←——————————————————————— Dining ———————————————————————→|

Arrears Brought Forward		Current Year Subs Etc		September		November		January		March		May	
	Pd		Pd		Pd		Pd		Pd		Pd		Pd
25	00												
17	00												
25	00												
8	50												
75	50												

Cash Book folio 1 — Exborough Lodge Analysed Cash Book

Date	Details	Initiation Joining Rejoining	Sub-scriptions	Dining	Contra	Bank	Date	Details	Cheq N
1986							1986		
September 1	Balance				450 00	450 00			
5	B. Baker		25 00				September 9	Exborough Masonic Hall	00
	D. Desmond		25 00			50 00		Exborough Caterers	00
10	A. Abel		25 00	8 50				S Symon (Tyler)	00
	C. Charley			8 50			15	Modern Printers (Summonses)	00
	E. Eagle		25 00	8 50			October 21	QCCC	00
	F. Forsythe		25 00	17 00				Grand Lodge – Fee	00
	H. Henry		20 00	17 00			November 11	Exborough Masonic Hall	00
	J. Jones			8 50				Exborough Caterers	00
	M. Merry		25 00	8 50				S Symon (Tyler)	00
	N. Newman			8 50			17	Exborough Masonic Hall	01
	P. Peters		25 00	8 50				Raymonds Masonic – Rituals	01
	R. Rogers	60 00	25 00	25 50		349 00	December 10	Grand Lodge – Dues	01
17	D. Desmond			25 50				Province – Dues	01
	G. Gordon		25 00	8 50			1987		
	K. King			8 50			January 12	Exborough Masonic Hall	01
	N. Newman		25 00			92 50		Exborough Caterers	01
November 12	C. Charley		25 00	17 00				S Symon (Tyler)	01
	A. Abel			8 50			14	Raymonds Masonic – Regalia	01
	B. Baker			8 50			February 16	Exborough Masonic Hall	01
	D. Desmond			8 50			March 14	Exborough Masonic Hall	01
	E. Eagle			8 50				Exborough Caterers	02
	F. Forsythe			17 00				S Symon (Tyler) – Paid Cash	–
	G. Gordon			17 00			16	Raymond Masonic – Regalia	02
	H. Henry			8 50			April 15	J. Jones – Secretarial	02
	J. Jones			8 50			22	Exborough Masonic Hall	02
	K. King		25 00	25 50			10	Exborough Masonic Hall	02
	L. Love			25 50				Exborough Caterers	02
	M. Merry			8 50				S. Symon (Tyler)	02
	N. Newman			8 50				12	Lodge Benevolent Fund	02
	P. Peters			8 50		237 00	July 15	Modern Printers (Letterheads)	02
	R. Rogers			8 50					
18	B. Baker			17 00		17 00			
1987									
January 14	A. Abel			17 00					
	B. Baker			8 50					
	C. Charley			8 50					
	D. Desmond			8 50					
	E. Eagle			8 50	2 00				
	F. Forsythe			8 50					
	G. Gordon			17 00					
	c/f	60 00	320 00	442 00	452 00	1195 50			

78

nk	Grand Lodge	Provincial Grand Lodge	Temple Hire	Regalia Etc	Printing Post & Stationery	Dining	Tyler	Contra	Miscellaneous	
3 50			18 50							
2 10						242 10				
00							8 00			
00					25 00					
00										
9 50	9 50								Quatuor Coronati-sub	8 00
50			18 50							
20						227 20				
00							8 00			
00										
00				25 00					Committee Room	5 00
2 72	82 72									
24		46 24								
50			18 50							
00						240 00				
00							8 00			
00				8 00				¢2 00		
00									Committee Room	5 00
50			18 50							
21						297 21				
00							8 00			
00				35 00						
00					15 00					
00									Committee Room	5 00
50			18 50							
50						241 50				
00							8 00			
00								30 00		
00					10 00					
97	92 22	46 24	92 50	68 00	50 00	1248 01	40 00	32 00		23 00

Cash Book folio 2

Date	Details	Initiation Joining Rejoining	Sub-scriptions	Dining	Contra	Bank	Date	Details
1987							1987	
	Brought Forward	60 00	320 00	442 00	452 00	1195 50		Brought forward
January 14	H. Henry			8 50				Balance c/
	J. Jones			8 50				
	K. King			8 50				
	L. Love			17 00				
	M. Merry			8 50				
	N. Newman			17 00				
	P. Peters			8 50				
	R. Rogers			8 50		163 50		
March 15	A. Abel			8 00		8 00		
	A. Abel			19 00				
	B. Baker			18 00				
	C. Charley			18 00				
	D. Desmond			9 00				
	E. Eagle			18 00				
	F. Forsyth			9 00				
	G. Gordon			45 00				
	H. Henry			27 00				
	J. Jones			18 00				
	K. King			27 00				
	L. Love			9 00				
	M. Merry			9 00				
	N. Newman			18 00				
	P. Peters			27 00				
	R. Rogers			9 00		280 00		
May 12	A. Abel			8 50				
	B. Baker			8 50				
	C. Charley			8 50				
	D. Desmond			17 00				
	E. Eagle			8 50				
	F. Forsyth			17 00				
	G. Gordon			8 50				
	H. Henry			8 50				
	J. Jones			8 50				
	L. Love			8 50				
	M. Merry			17 00				
	N. Newman			17 00				
	R. Rogers			25 50		161 50		
	Benevolent Fund							
	Cash				30 00	30 00		
		60 00	320 00	976 50	482 00	1838 50		
		NL/1	NL/2	NL/3	Contra 32 00			
					Balance 450 00			
					£482 00			

Cash Book folio 2 *contd.*

ue	Bank	Grand Lodge	Provincial Grand Lodge	Temple Hire	Regalia Etc	Printing Post & Stationery	Dining	Tyler	Contra	Miscellaneous	
	1691 97	92 22	46 24	92 50	68 00	50 00	1248 01	40 00	32 00		
	146 53								146 53		23 00
	1838 50	92 22	46 24	92 50	68 00	50 00	1248 01	40 00	178 53		23 00
		NL/4	NL/5	NL/6	NL/7	NL/8	NL/3	NL/9		Subscription NL/10	8 00
								Contra	32 00		15 00
								Balance	146 53	Committee Rooms NL/11	23 00
									£178 53		

Cash Book folio 3

Date	Details	Initiation Joining Rejoining		Sub-scriptions		Dining		Contra		Bank		Date	Details	C
1987 September 1	Balance B/F							146	53	146	53			

Cash Book folio 3 *contd.*

ank	Grand Lodge		Provincial Grand Lodge		Temple Hire		Regalia Etc		Printing Post & Stationery		Dining		Tyler		Contra		Miscel-laneous		

Exborough Lodge No. XXXX

Books of Account

A/C No. 1

Initiation Joining and Rejoining Fees
A/C No. 1

				1987			
				August 31	Bank	CB/2	60 00

A/C No. 2
Subscriptions
A/C No. 2

1986				1987			
Sep 1	Balance	B/f	20 00	Aug 31	Bank	CB/2	320 00

A/C No. 3
Dining
A/C No. 3

1987				1987			
Aug 31	Bank	CB/2	1248 01	Aug 31	Bank	CB/2	976 50
	Caterers				*Received*		
	Charges				*from*		
					members		

A/C No. 4
Grand Lodge – Dues
A/C No. 4

1987							
Aug 31	Bank	CB/2	92 22				

A/C No. 5
Provincial Grand Lodge – Dues
A/C No. 5

1987							
Aug 31	Bank	CB/2	46 24				

Appendix 1

A/C No. 6				**A/C No. 6**
		Temple Hire		
1987				
Aug 31	Bank	CB/2	92 50	

A/C No. 7				**A/C No. 7**
		Regalia, etc		
1987				
Aug 31	Bank			
	(Rituals			
	£25)	CB/2	68 00	
	(Regalia			
	£43)			

A/C No. 8				**A/C No. 8**
		Printing Postage and Stationery		
1987				
Aug 31	Bank	CB/2	50 00	

A/C No. 9				**A/C No. 9**
		Tylers Fees		
1987				
Aug 31	Bank	CB/2	40 00	

A/C No. 10				**A/C No. 10**
		QCCC Subscription		
1987				
Aug 31	Bank	CB/2	8 00	

A/C No. 11				**A/C No. 11**
		Committee Expenses		
1987				
Aug 31	Bank	CB/2	15 00	

A/C No. 12   **A/C No. 12**

Exborough Masonic Hall Company – Shares

1987			
Aug 31	Bank – 500 £1 Shares	CB/10	500 00

A/C No. 13   **A/C No. 13**

Accumulated Fund

1986			
Sep 1	Balance	B/F	970 00

A/C No. 14   **A/C No. 14**

Insurance

APPENDIX 2

Appendix 2

The Extended Trial Balance

Trial Balance (1)

			Dr	Cr
NL	1	Initiation Joining & Rejoining Fees		60 00
	2	Subscriptions		300 00
	3	Dining	1248 01	976 50
	4	Grand Lodge Dues	92 22	
	5	Provincial Grand Lodge Dues	46 24	
	6	Temple Hire	92 50	
	7	Regalia etc.	68 00	
	8	Printing Postage & Staionery	50 00	
	9	Tylers Fees	40 00	
	10	QCCC Subscription	8 00	
	11	Committee Expenses	15 00	
	12	Exborough Masonic Hall Company—Dues	500 00	
	13	Accumulated Fund		970 00
		Balance at Bank for Cash Book	146 53	
			2306 50	2306 50

Extended

NL			Dr	Cr	
	1	Initiation Joining & Rejoing Fees		60 00	
	2	Subscriptions		300 00	
	3	Dining	1248 01	976 50	
	4	Grand Lodge Dues	92 22		
	5	Provincial Grand Lodge Dues	46 24		
	6	Temple Hire	92 50		
	7	Regalia etc.	68 00		
	8	Printing Postage & Stationery	50 00		
	9	Tylers Fees	40 00		
	10	QCCC Subscription	8 00		
	11	Committee Expenses	15 00		
	12	Exborough Masonic Hall Company—Dues	500 00		
	13	Accumulated Fund		970 00	
		Insurance			
		Balance at Bank for Cash Book	146 53		
		Debtors/Creditors			
		Surplus/Deficit			
			2306 50	2306 50	

ce (2)

	Dr Creditors	Cr Debtors		Income & Dr	Expenditure Cr	Balance Dr	Sheet Cr
					60 00		
		50 00			350 00		
		25 50		1248 01	1002 00		
				92 22			
				46 24			
				92 50			
				68 00			
				50 00			
				40 00			
				8 00			
				15 00			
						500 00	
							970 00
	2 00			2 00			
						146 53	
						75 50	2 00
					249 97	249 97	
	2 00	75 50		1661 97	1661 97	972 00	972 00

Extended Trial Balance (3)

	Opening Balances		Cash Book		Transfers
	Dr.	Cr.	Dr.	Cr.	Dr
Subscriptions	20 00			320 00	
Shares in Masonic Hall Company	500 00				
Accumulated Fund		970 00			
Bank	450 00		1386 50	1689 97	
Initiation Joining & Rejoining				60 00	
Dining			1248 01	976 50	
Contras			30 00	30 00	
Grand Lodge Dues			92 22		
Provincial Grand Lodge Dues			46 24		
Temple Hire			92 50		
Regalia Etc.			68 00		
Printing, Postage and Stationary			50 00		
Tyler			40 00		
QCCC Subscription			8 00		
Committee Rooms			15 00		
Insurance					
Debtors/Creditors					
Surplus (Deficit)					
	970 00	970 00	3076 47	3076 47	

Cr	Dr. Creditors	Cr. Debtors		Income & Expenditure Dr.	Cr.	Balance Sheet Dr.	Cr.
		50 00			350 00	500 00	
							970 00
						146 53	
		25 50		1248 01	60 00		
					1002 00		
				92 22			
				46 24			
				92 50			
				68 00			
				50 00			
				40 00			
				8 00			
				15 00			
	2 00			2 00			
						75 50	2 00
					249 97	249 97	
	2 00	75 50		1661 97	1661 97	972 00	972 00

APPENDIX 3

The Final Accounts of The Exborough Lodge

Exborough Lodge No XXXX

Income and Expenditure Account – year to 31st August 1987

Income

Initiation Fees	60.00
Subscriptions	350.00
	410.00

Expenditure

Dues	Grand Lodge	92.22
	Provisional Grand Lodge	46.24
	Total Dues	138.46

Meetings	Dining	1248.01
	Less: receipts	1002.00
	Net dining costs	246.01
	Temple hire	92.50
	Tylers Fees	40.00
	Total Meeting Costs	378.51

Administration Costs

Printing, postage and stationary	50.00
Insurance	2.00
Committee Rooms	15.00
Subscription	8.00
Regatta	43.00
Rituals	25.00
Total Administration Costs	143.00

Total Expenditure	659.97
Excess of Expenditure over Income for the year	£249.97

Exborough Lodge No XXXX
Balance Sheet at 31st August 1987

Fixed Assets

500 £1 shares in Exborough Masonic Hall Ltd.		500.00

Current Assets

Debtors (subscriptions and joining fees	75.50	
Balance at bank	146.53	
	222.03	
Deduct: Creditor	2.00	
Net Current Assets		220.03
		£720.03

Accumulated Fund

Balance at 1st September 1986		970.00
Deduct: Excess of Expenditure of the year		249.97
		£720.03

Initiation Joining and Rejoing Fees

A/c No. 1

1987				1987			
Aug 31	Income & Expenditure A/c		*60.00*	Aug 31	Bank	CB/2	60.00

Subscriptions

A/c No. 2

1987				1987			
Sept 1	Balance	B/f	20.00	Aug 31	Bank	CB/2	320.00
Aug 31	Income & Expenditure A/c		*350.00*		Balance	c/d	*50.00*
			370.00				370.00

1987							
Sept 1	Balance	B/d	50.00				

Dining

A/c No. 3

1987				1987			
Aug 31	Caterers Charges	CB/2	1248.00	Aug 31	Bank		
	Income & Expenditure A/c		*1002.00*		Rec.d from Members		976.50
					Income & Expenditure A/C		*1248.01*
					Balance c/d		25.50
			2250.01				2250.01

1987							
Sept 1	Balance	B/d	25.50				

Grand Lodge – Dues

A/c No. 4

1987				1987			
Aug 31	Bank	CB/2	92.22	Aug 31	Income & Expenditure A/C		*92.22*

Provincial Grand Lodge – Dues

A/c No. 5

1987				1987		
Aug 31	Bank	CB/2	46.24	Aug 31	Income & Expenditure A/C	46.24

Temple Hire

A/c No. 6

1987				1987		
Aug 31	Bank	CB/2	92.50	Aug 31	Income & Expenditure A/C	92.50

Regalia Etc.

A/c No. 7

1987				1987		
Aug 31	Bank (Rituals £25) (Regalia £43)	CB/2	68.00	Aug 31	Income & Expenditure A/C	68.00

Printing, Postage and Stationary

A/c No. 8

1987				1987		
Aug 31	Bank	CB/2	50.00	Aug 31	Income & Expenditure A/C	50.00

Tylers Fees

A/c No. 9

1987				1987		
Aug 31	Bank	CB/2	40.00	Aug 31	Income & Expenditure A/C	40.00

QCCC Subscription

A/c No. 10

1987				1987		
Aug 31	Bank	CB/2	8.00	Aug 31	Income & Expenditure A/C	8.00

Committee Expenses

A/c No. 11

1987				1987		
Aug 31	Bank		15.00	Aug 31	Income & Expenditure A/C	15.00

Exborough Memorial Hall Company – Shares

A/c No. 12

1985		
Aug 31	Bank – 500 £1 Share	500.00

Accumulated Fund

A/c No. 13

1987				1986			
Aug 31	Deficiency transferred from Income & Expenditure A/c		249.97	Sept 1	Balance	b/f	970.00
	Balance	c/d	720.03				
			970.00				970.00
				1987			
				Sept 1	Balance	b/f	720.03

Insurance

A/c No. 14

1987				1987		
Aug 31	Balance	c/f	2.00	Aug 31	Inc. & Expenditure A/C	2.00
				1987		
				Sept 1	Balance	b/d	2.00

APPENDIX 4

Charitable Trusts

THIS DECLARATION OF TRUST is made the
day of   One thousand nine hundred and
BY   in the County of
and   of   hereinafter
called "the Trustees" which expression shall include the trustees
or trustee for the time being hereof ————————————

WHEREAS:

(1) It is intended to establish amongst the members
from time to time of the   Lodge (hereinafter
called "the Lodge") a charitable fund to be called
The   Lodge Benevolent Trust (hereinafter called
"the Charity") ————————————————

(2) The Trustees are the trustees of the Charity
NOW THIS DEED WITNESSETH AND IT IS
HEREBY DECLARED as follows:–

1. The objects of the Charity shall be the relief of poverty the
advancement of education the advancement of religion and
other purposes beneficial to the community provided the same
are exclusively charitable purposes within the meaning of the
law of England and Wales ————————————————

2. The Trustees shall apply all or any part of the monies received whether by way of subscription donation bequest or otherwise for any or all of the objects of the Charity as hereinbefore defined in accordance with the directions from time to time given by a simple majority of the members of the Lodge _____

3. All monies from time to time held by the Trustees on behalf of the Charity shall be kept in a separate bank account in the name of the Charity with   Bank Limited or such other Bank as the Lodge may from time to time by a simple majority determine _____

4. The Trustees shall have power (but shall not be obliged) to invest any sums held undistributed from time to time in such investments as shall from time to time be permitted by law for the investment of trust funds subject to the prior approval of any such investments by a simple majority of members of the Lodge present and voting at any meeting of the Lodge _____

5. The Trustees of this deed shall hold office until the   day of   next and thereafter the trustees from time to time of this deed shall hold office for one year from the first day of   in each year The Trustees shall be Three in number and shall consist of the Worshipful Master, the Treasurer and the Secretary for the time being of the Lodge. Any occasional vacancy which may occur shall be filled by a Past Master to be elected by a simple majority at any meeting of the Lodge and the person elected to

fill any such vacancy shall hold office until the
day of   next following _____

6. The Lodge Secretary for the time being shall act as Hon
Secretary of the Charity _____

7. The books of the Charity shall be audited annually by
the Hon Auditors appointed to audit the books of the
Lodge _____

8. The Trustees shall keep proper books of account and a
minute book which shall be open for inspection at all times by
the Committee of the Lodge and the Lodge's Hon Auditors
and by such other persons as the Committee of the Lodge may
from time to time nominate _____

9. The Trustees may from time to time by writing under their
hands authorise any two or more of the Trustees to sign or
endorse on their behalf any cheques bills negotiable instru-
ments or contracts and every such authority shall continue in
force until some one or more of the Trustees shall by writing
under his or their hand or hands retract the same and
communicate such revocation to the person holding such
authority _____

10. The Trustees (which expression for the purpose of this
clause includes any of them) shall not be liable for the
consequences of any error forgetfulness or omission whether of
law or of fact on the part of any of the Trustees or their
advisers or generally for any breach of duty or trust what-

soever unless it shall be proved to have been committed given or omitted in personal conscious bad faith by the Trustee charged to be so liable _____

IN WITNESS whereof the parties hereto have hereto set their hands and Seals the day and year first above written _____

SIGNED SEALED and DELIVERED
by the said

        in the presence of

SIGNED SEALED and DELIVERED
by the said

        in the presence of

SIGNED SEALED and DELIVERED
by the said

        in the presence of

THIS DEED OF COVENANT is made the
day of   19   BETWEEN   of
                  (hereinafter called "the Subscriber") of the one
part and   (hereinafter called "the Charity") of the
other part:
WHEREAS the Subscriber is desirous of binding himself to
support the Charity and its work by entering into the covenant
hereafter contained;
NOW THIS DEED WITNESSETH as follows:
The Subscriber hereby covenants with the Charity that he will
during the term of   years from the date hereof
or during his lifetime (whichever is the shorter period) pay to
the funds of the Charity annually out of his taxed income
such a sum as will after deduction of income tax at the basic
rate for the time being in force leave a sum of
pounds (£   )

In witness whereof I have
hereunto affixed my hand
and Seal the date and year
first above written

Witness
....
....
....
....

Exborough Lodge No. XXXX
Benevolent Trust Covenanted Income Record

No.	Name	Net Annual Sum	First Year	Final Year	May		September	
1.	A. Abel	5 00	1987/88	1990/91	1 00	12/5	1 00	8/9

| 1987/88 | | | | | | May | September | 1988/89 | | | | March | |
November		January		March				November		January			
1 00	4/11	1 00	12/1	1 00	8/3								

NOTES

NOTES

NOTES